Langenscheidt

Murder! Murder? Murder!

Englische und amerikanische Thriller mit Übersetzungshilfen

Langenscheidt

Berlin · München · Wien · Zürich · New York

www.langenscheidt.de

Druck: Mercedes-Druck GmbH, Berlin
Printed in Germany

ISBN-13: 978-3-468-44425-8
ISBN-10: 3-468-44425-7

3. 4. 5. 6. 7. * 10 09 08 07 06

Vorwort

Die fünf Erzählungen dieses Bandes sind keine Kriminalgeschichten im üblichen Sinne. Es sind zwar „Mordgeschichten", aber die vorliegende Auswahl zeigt, dass es nicht immer nur Detektive und Kriminalbeamte sein müssen, die für die zusätzliche Spannung sorgen. Zwar bleibt die Fragestellung „Wer ist der Schuldige?", aber weniger Motiv und Tat als vielmehr die Persönlichkeit von Täter und Opfer stehen im Vordergrund jeder dieser ungewöhnlichen Geschichten.

Zwei Autoren schienen uns für diesen Band besonders geeignet zu sein, Dorothy L. Sayers und Edgar Allan Poe: Dorothy Sayers – neben Agatha Christie wohl die bedeutendste Autorin von Kriminalromanen in England – weil sie von jeher bemüht war, durch überzeugende Charaktere die Mechanisierung des Detektivromans zu überwinden; Edgar Allan Poe, weil er als Vorläufer des heutigen logisch deduzierenden Kriminalromans kriminalistischen Scharfblick mit dem Hang zum Phantastischen und Unheimlichen verbindet. Dorothy Sayers sagt über Poe und die Etablierung des Kriminalromans als Literaturgattung; "The ball – the original nucleus deposited by Edgar Allan Poe … – was at last set rolling. As it went, it swelled into a vast mass – it set off others – it became a spate – a torrent – an avalanche of mystery fiction."

Aber auch Humor und englischer Spleen kommen in zwei Geschichten anderer Autoren zu Wort. Alles in allem, wie wir hoffen, eine gelungene Mischung spannender Geschichten aus dem reichen Schatz dieser Literaturgattung.

Langenscheidt

Inhaltsverzeichnis

Erklärung der Lautschrift

A Vokale und Diphthonge

[ɑː] reines langes a, wie in Vater, kam, Schwan: *far* [fɑː], *father* ['fɑːðə].

[ʌ] kommt im Deutschen nicht vor. Kurzes dunkles a, bei dem die Lippen nicht gerundet sind. Vorn und offen gebildet: *butter* ['bʌtə], *come* [kʌm], *colour* ['kʌlə], *blood* [blʌd], *flourish* ['flʌrɪʃ], *twopence* ['tʌpəns].

[æ] heller, ziemlich offener, nicht zu kurzer a-Laut, wie das kurze a in Quatsch oder waschen: *fat* [fæt], *man* [mæn].

[eə] nicht zu offenes halb langes ä; im Englischen nur vor r, das als ein dem ä nachhallendes ə erscheint: *bare* [beə], *pair* [peə], *there* [ðeə].

[aɪ] Bestandteile: helles, zwischen ɑː und æ liegendes a und schwächeres offenes i. Die Zunge hebt sich halbwegs zur i-Stellung: *I* [aɪ], *lie* [laɪ], *dry* [draɪ].

[aʊ] Bestandteile: helles, zwischen ɑː und æ liegendes a und schwächeres offenes u: *house* [haʊs], *now* [naʊ].

[eɪ] halb offenes e, nach i auslautend, indem die Zunge sich halbwegs zur i-Stellung hebt: *date* [deɪt], *play* [pleɪ], *obey* [ə'beɪ].

[e] halb offenes kurzes e, etwas geschlossener als das e in Bett: *bed* [bed], *less* [les].

[ə] flüchtiger Gleitlaut, ähnlich dem deutschen, flüchtig gesprochenen e in Gelage: *about* [ə'baʊt], *butter* ['bʌtə], *connect* [kə'nekt].

[iː] langes i, wie in lieb, Bibel, aber etwas offener einsetzend als im Deutschen; wird in Südengland doppellautig gesprochen, indem sich die Zunge allmählich zur i-Stellung hebt: *scene* [siːn], *sea* [siː], *feet* [fiːt], *ceiling* ['siːlɪŋ].

[ɪ] kurzes offenes i wie in bin, mit: *big* [bɪg], *city* ['sɪtɪ].

[ɪə] halb offenes halb langes i mit nachhallendem ə: *here* [hɪə], *hear* [hɪə], *inferior* [ɪn'fɪərɪə].

[əʊ] mit [ə] beginnend und in schwaches u auslautend, keine Rundung der Lippen, kein Heben der Zunge: *note* [nəʊt], *boat* [bəʊt], *below* [bɪ'ləʊ].

[ɔː] offener langer, zwischen a und o schwebender Laut: *fall* [fɔːl], *nought* [nɔːt], *or* [ɔː], *before* [bɪ'fɔː].

[ɒ] offener kurzer, zwischen a und o schwebender Laut, offener als das o in Motte: *god* [gɒd], *not* [nɒt], *wash* [wɒʃ], *hobby* ['hɒbɪ].

[ɔɪ] Bestandteile: offenes o und schwächeres offenes i. Die Zunge hebt sich halbwegs zur i-Stellung: *voice* [vɔɪs], *boy* [bɔɪ], *annoy* [ə'nɔɪ].

[ɜː] im Deutschen fehlender Laut; offenes langes ö, etwa wie gedehnt gesprochenes ö in öffnen, Mörder; kein Vorstülpen oder Runden der Lippen; kein Heben der Zunge: *word* [wɜːd], *girl* [gɜːl], *learn* [lɜːn], *murmur* ['mɜːmə].

[uː] langes u wie in Buch, doch ohne Lippenrundung; vielfach diphthongisch als halb offenes langes u mit nachhallendem geschlossenem u: *fool* [fuːl], *shoe* [ʃuː], *you* [juː], *rule* [ruːl], *canoe* [kə'nuː].

[ʊə] halb offenes halb langes u mit nachhallendem ə: *poor* [pʊə], *sure* [ʃʊə], *allure* [ə'ljʊə].

[ʊ] flüchtiges u: *put* [pʊt], *look* [lʊk], *careful* ['keəfʊl].

Ganz vereinzelt werden auch die folgenden französischen Laute gebraucht: Die Nasale [ɑ̃] wie in frz. *blanc,* [ɔ̃] wie in frz. *bonbon* und [ɛ̃] wie in frz. *vin,* sowie die drei Vokale [o] wie in frz. *chaud,* [ɛ] wie in frz. *belle* und [ø] wie in frz. *monsieur.*

Die **Länge eines Vokals** wird durch [ː] bezeichnet, z.B. *ask* [ɑːsk], *astir* [ə'stɜː]. Die **Betonung** der englischen Wörter wird durch das Zeichen ['] vor der zu betonenden Silbe angegeben, z.B. *onion* ['ʌnjən].

B Konsonanten

[r] nur vor Vokalen gesprochen. Völlig verschieden vom deutschen Zungenspitzen- oder Zäpfchen-r. Die Zungenspitze bildet mit der oberen Zahnwulst eine Enge, durch die der Ausatmungsstrom mit Stimmton hindurchgetrieben wird, ohne den Laut zu rollen. Am Ende eines Wortes wird r nur bei Bindung mit dem Anlautvokal des folgenden Wortes gesprochen; *rose* [rəʊz], *pride* [praɪd], *there is* [ðeər'ɪz].

[ʒ] stimmhaftes sch, wie g in Genie, j in Journal: *azure* ['æʒə], *jazz* [dʒæz], *jeep* [dʒiːp], *large* [lɑːdʒ].

[ʃ] stimmloses sch, wie im Deutschen Schnee, rasch: *shake* [ʃeɪk], *washing* ['wɒʃɪŋ], *lash* [læʃ].

[θ] im Deutschen nicht vorhandener stimmloser Lispellaut; durch Anlegen der Zunge an die oberen Schneidezähne hervorgebracht: *thin* [θɪn], *path* [pɑːθ], *method* ['meθəd].

[ð] derselbe Laut stimmhaft, d.h. mit Stimmton: *there* [ðeə], *breathe* [briːð], *father* ['fɑːðə].

[s] stimmloser Zischlaut, entsprechend dem deutschen ß in Spaß, reißen: *see* [siː], *hats* [hæts], *decide* [dɪ'saɪd].

[z] stimmhafter Zischlaut wie im Deutschen sausen: *zeal* [ziːl], *rise* [raɪz], *horizon* [hə'raɪzn].

[ŋ] wird wie der deutsche Nasenlaut in fangen, singen gebildet: *ring* [rɪŋ], *singer* ['sɪŋə].

[ŋk] derselbe Laut mit nachfolgendem k wie im Deutschen senken, Wink: *ink* [ɪŋk], *tinker* ['tɪŋkə].

[w] flüchtiges, mit Lippe an Lippe gesprochenes w, aus der Mundstellung für uː gebildet: *will* [wɪl], *swear* [sweə], *queen* [kwiːn].

[f] stimmloser Lippenlaut wie im Deutschen flott: *fat* [fæt], *tough* [tʌf], *effort* ['efət].

[v] stimmhafter Lippenlaut wie im Deutschen Vase, Ventil: *vein* [veɪn], *velvet* ['velvɪt].

[j] flüchtiger zwischen j und i schwebender Laut: *onion* ['ʌnjən], *yes* [jes], *filial* ['fɪljəl].

Verwendete Abkürzungen

Abkzg	Abkürzung
AE	amerikanisches Englisch
BE	britisches Englisch
bes.	besonders
e-e	eine
e-r	einer
e-s	eines
et.	etwas
F	Familiär (= Umgangssprache)
j-d	jemand
j-m	jemandem
j-n	jemanden
j-s	jemandes
m-e	meine
m-r	meiner
m-s	meines
od.	oder
o.s.	oneself
Pl	Plural
s-e	seine
s-r	seiner
s-s	seines
Sg	Singular
sl.	Slang
s.o.	someone
s.th.	something
u.	und

Wir danken den folgenden Verlagen und Agenturen für Abdruckgenehmigungen:

Elek Books Ltd und David Higham Associates, Ltd für "The Fountain Plays" von Dorothy L. Sayers (aus der Sammlung "Murder Mixture").

Curtis Brown Ltd für "A Lesson in Crime" von G. D. H. und M. Cole.

Through The Window

By *K. R. G. Browne*

At the corner by Lord's **Cricket Ground** I paused to light a cigarette and give thanks to **Providence for my lack of a wife**. For the hour—if the clock above the Underground station was to be believed—was four-fifteen of a bright June morning, and I was **homeward bound** from an evening which had begun well with a **regimental dinner** and ended **riotously** with a poker-party in Bat Farquhar's flat. An evening of wine, **reminiscence**, anecdote and song—an evening, in short, such as your **Benedict** enjoys only at the risk of **subsequent** domestic **tribulation**. But I, being no woman's **chattel**, had no reason to dread the future or **rack my brains** for incredible excuses; and though—like every man—I was not without my own particular and private troubles, at the moment these **weighed upon** me not at all, for I was in that **mellow frame of mind** which comes of an **admirable** meal, much good discourse and a **measure of luck** with the cards. And so it was that, as I crossed the road and **plunged into** the **decorous byways** of St. John's Wood, I was **constrained** to sing a little, by way of welcome to the dawn.

---

cricket ground ['krɪkɪt graund] Kricketplatz **providence** ['prɒvɪdəns] Vorsehung **... for my lack of a wife** [læk, waɪf] dafür, dass ich keine (Ehe)Frau habe **homeward bound** ['həʊmwəd baʊnd] auf dem Heimweg **regimental dinner** [redʒɪ'mentl 'dɪnə] hier: Essen m-s Regiments **riotous** ['raɪətəs] ausgelassen **reminiscence** [remɪ'nɪsns] Erinnerung **benedict** ['benɪdɪkt] = **benedick** ['benedɪk] frischgebackener Ehemann **subsequent** ['sʌbsɪkwənt] folgend, später **tribulation** [trɪbjʊ'leɪʃn] Leiden **chattel** ['tʃætl] Sklave **rack one's brains** [ræk, breɪnz] sich den Kopf zermartern **weigh upon** [weɪ] hier: belasten **mellow** F ['meləʊ] heiter **frame of mind** [freɪm, maɪnd] Gemütsverfassung **admirable** ['ædmərəbl] großartig **measure of luck** ['meʒə, lʌk] Portion Glück **plunge into** [plʌndʒ] stürmen in, plötzlich betreten **decorous** ['dekərəs] (wohl)anständig **byway** ['baɪweɪ] Nebenstraße **be constrained to do s.th.** [kən'streɪnd] sich gezwungen fühlen, et. zu tun

And why not? If a man may not sing on his way home from a regimental dinner, when may he sing? I would not have it thought, **mind you**, that I sang loudly in a **raucous** voice, to the **discomfort** of the neighbourhood. Not so. I sang softly in a gentlemanly tenor, robbing no man of his rest. As for the **purport** of my song, **that is neither here nor there**; it is enough to say that it was a ballad of the kind that may **with impunity** be sung at dawn in St. John's Wood, or at high noon in the Sahara, or at midnight in Alaska, but never in a **drawing-room** at tea-time by one **having a regard** for the conventions. A manly and comforting song, if you follow me, but somewhat limited in its **appeal**.

It was as I **embarked upon** the eleventh and **penultimate** verse of this song that I turned the corner into **Laburnum** Road, N.W.8, and saw before me a policeman. And at sight of that large blue shape my song **perished** suddenly within me, for there is something about policemen that **paralyses** my **vocal cords**, even after a regimental dinner and a measure of luck with the cards.

This was a very high, very broad, very **efficient-looking** policeman, and he stood upon the **kerb** near the corner, rocking gently back and forth upon his heels and **gazing pensively** into infinity, as policemen will when there are no murderers or motorists available for their **diversion**. As I ap-

---

mind you wohlgemerkt! **raucous** ['rɔːkəs] rau, heiser **discomfort** [dɪs'kʌmfət] Verdruss **purport** ['pɜːpət] Inhalt, Sinn **that is neither here nor there** ['naɪðə, nɔː] das gehört nicht zur Sache **with impunity** [ɪm'pjuːnɪtɪ] ungestraft **drawing-room** ['drɔɪŋrʊm] Salon **have a regard for** [rɪ'gɑːd] Rücksicht nehmen auf **appeal** [ə'piːl] Anklang, Wirkung **embark upon** [ɪm'bɑːk] anfangen **penultimate** [pɪ'nʌltɪmɪt] vorletzt **laburnum** [lə'bɜːnəm] Goldregen **perish** ['perɪʃ] zugrunde gehen, sterben **paralyse** ['pærəlaɪz] lähmen **vocal cords** Pl ['vəʊkəl kɔːdz] Stimmbänder **efficient-looking** [ɪ'fɪʃnt'lʊkɪŋ] tüchtig aussehend **kerb BE** [kɜːb] Bordstein **gaze** [geɪz] starren **pensive** ['pensɪv] nachdenklich **diversion** [daɪ'vɜːʃn] Zeitvertreib, Unterhaltung **survey** [sɜː'veɪ] mustern

proached, he turned slowly and **surveyed** me in a mildly interested way, much as a **naturalist** might survey a beetle of whose exact species he was a little doubtful. I observed that he had a **keen** blue eye and very red hair and a chin like the toe of a football boot; and I noted also that he was a **comparatively juvenile** policeman, being of my own age or **thereabouts**.

Now, **ordinarily** it is not my way to **engage** policemen **in conversation**. My **conscience** is as **tranquil** as that of the average man, but policemen **awe** me, because they are such **lofty** folk. I myself am of no great stature, and it is somehow **humiliating** to have to lean back and talk up at a man, after the fashion of a tourist examining the Eiffel Tower. But on this morning, as it happened, I was feeling **conversationally inclined**, for I will not **deny** that good wine has the effect of **unshackling** my tongue, as any of my relations would be only too willing to **testify**. And it seemed to me, too, that this was a rather bored and melancholy policeman, and that it was my **plain** duty as a **taxpaying** citizen to **cheer** him with a kindly word. Nothing on earth, you understand, would have **induced** me to sing to him, but **mere courtesy forbade** me to pass him by without a word of greeting.

'Good morning, officer,' I said, having heard somewhere that it **gratifies** a policeman to be so addressed.

---

naturalist ['nætʃrəlɪst] Zoologe **keen** [kiːn] scharf **comparatively** [kəm'pærətɪvlɪ] verhältnismäßig, ziemlich **juvenile** ['dʒuːvɪnaɪl] jung **thereabouts** ['ðeərəbaʊts] so etwa **ordinarily** ['ɔːdnrɪlɪ] gewöhnlich **engage s.o. in conversation** [ɪn'geɪdʒ, kɒnvə'seɪʃn] j-n ins Gespräch ziehen **conscience** ['kɒnʃns] Gewissen **tranquil** ['træŋkwɪl] ruhig **awe** [ɔː] einschüchtern **lofty** ['lɒftɪ] hochaufragend **humiliating** [hjuː'mɪlɪeɪtɪŋ] demütigend **feel conversationally inclined** [kɒnvə'seɪʃnəl, ɪn'klaɪnd] hier: nach Unterhaltung zumute sein **deny** [dɪ'naɪ] leugnen, verweigern **unshackle** ['ʌn'ʃækl] befreien, hier: lösen **testify** ['testɪfaɪ] bezeugen **plain** [pleɪn] einfach, eindeutig **taxpaying** ['tækspeɪɪŋ] steuerzahlend **cheer** [tʃɪə] aufheitern **induce** [ɪn'djuːs] bewegen **mere courtesy** [mɪə 'kɜːtɪsɪ] pure Höflichkeit **forbade** [fə'bæd] von **forbid** [fə'bɪd] verbieten **gratify** ['grætɪfaɪ] erfreuen

'Good morning,' answered the policeman; and if he was gratified, he did not show it.

'I've been to a party,' I said—not meaning to **boast**, but with intent to explain my presence in Laburnum Road at four-twenty of a bright June morning.

'Is that so?' said the policeman; and he looked thoughtfully at my **shirt-front**, whereon Bat Farquhar—ever a humorous **lad—had seen fit to** work out certain monetary problems with the help of an **indelible pencil**. Boys will be boys, and who am I to deny a friend his little harmless pleasures?

'They're being worn like that now, you know,' I said coughing **slightly**, and drawing my coat about me. 'A **jolly** day, don't you think?'

'Yes,' said the policeman.

It was becoming clear to me that this was not one of our more chatty policemen, but I thought no less of him **on that account**, for a night spent on the **beat** in Laburnum Road would **atrophy** any man's powers of conversation.

'Well,' I said, **keeping the ball rolling**, 'thanks very much for looking after Laburnum Road so nicely. It's a great **comfort** to know that I can go out any time and—'

'You live in this road?' said the policeman.

'I can't deny it,' I answered, 'At Number twenty. Any time you're passing—'

---

boast [bəʊst] prahlen, großtun **shirt-front** ['ʃɜːtfrʌnt] Hemdbrust **lad** [læd] Bursche, Junge **had seen fit** von **see fit** es für richtig halten **indelible pencil** [ɪn'delɪbl 'pensl] Tintenstift **slightly** ['slaɪtlɪ] schwach, etwas **jolly** ['dʒɒlɪ] famos, herrlich **on that account** [ə'kaʊnt] deswegen **beat** [biːt] Runde (e-s Polizisten) **atrophy** ['ætrəfɪ] verkümmern lassen **keep the ball rolling** das Gespräch in Gang halten **comfort** ['kʌmfət] Beruhigung

'Ah,' said the policeman. 'Then do you know who lives in that house over there?' And he pointed to a house that faced us across the road; an **excessively neat** little house in a **painfully** neat little garden; a **smug** little house of the **double-fronted** sort, **lace-curtained**, **brass-knockered** and wearing a **lamentable aspidistra** in its lower left-hand window.

'Number Four?' said I. 'That is the home of our Mr. Alaric Thrall. Do you want to be introduced?'

'A friend of yours?' said the policeman.

'No friend of mine,' said I, 'nor of any man, so far as I know.'

'Ah,' said the policeman, and for a space considered me **in an absent-minded sort of way**. 'I've been wondering why that window's open, that's all.'

Now that my **attention** was drawn to the matter, I **perceived** that one of Mr.Thrall's windows was **indubitably** open. The window of a room upon the ground floor, to the right of the neat green door.

'Officer,' I said admiringly, 'you've an eye like a **hawk**. But it is hardly for us to question Mr. Thrall's right to open his windos **as and when he chooses**.'

'That's true enough,' said the policeman mildly. 'But this is a **queer** sort of time to open windows, it seems to me.

---

excessive [ɪk'sesɪv] übertrieben **neat** [niːt] ordentlich, gepflegt **painfully** ['peɪnfʊlɪ] peinlich, übertrieben **smug** [smʌg] schmuck **double-fronted** ['dʌblfrʌntɪd] mit zwei Vorderfronten **lace-curtained** ['leɪskɜːtnd] mit Spitzengardinen **brass-knockered** ['brɑːsnɒkəd] mit e-m Türklopfer aus Messing **lamentable** ['læməntəbl] erbärmlich, kläglich **aspidistra** [æspɪ'dɪstrə] Aspidistra, Schildblume **in an absent-minded sort of way** ['æbsənt'maɪndɪd] wie geistesabwesend od. zerstreut **attention** [ə'tenʃn] Aufmerksamkeit **perceive** [pə'siːv] wahrnehmen, (be)merken **indubitable** [ɪn'djuːbɪtəbl] zweifel-, fraglos **hawk** [hɔːk] Falke **as and when he chooses** ['tʃuːzɪz] wie u. wann es ihm beliebt **queer** [kwɪə] sonderbar

When I passed this way twenty minutes ago that window was shut. And why,' said the policeman to nobody in particular, 'a *downstairs* window?'

I **pondered** the matter.

'A sudden **whim**, perhaps?' I suggested **deferentially**. 'I shouldn't have thought that Mr. Thrall was **much of a one for** fresh air—in fact, this is the first time I've ever seen any of his windows open—but you never can tell. He is a gentleman of eccentric **habits**, I understand, and he **keeps odd hours**. He lives there alone, you know, and his servants come in every morning. That room is his **study**, and if—'

I became aware that the keen blue eye of the policeman was looking at and through me.

'You seem,' said the policeman, 'to know a good deal about him. I thought you said he wasn't a friend of yours.'

'I did,' I agreed, 'and that was perfectly true. Between you and me and my shirt-front, officer, I don't mind saying that if I were asked to choose between Mr. Thrall and a one-eyed, three-legged **mongrel pup** with **distemper**, I'd go and buy a **dog-licence** at once. But I know him, **none the less**. At least, I've met him. Quite a lot of people have met Mr. Thrall, but he hasn't many friends, I think.'

'Is that so?' said the policeman, in a far-away voice. And after a little pause: 'Well, that window looks a bit queer to me.'

---

ponder ['pɒndə] nachdenken über **whim** [wɪm] Laune, Marotte **deferential** [defə'renʃl] ehrerbietig, respektvoll **be much of a one for** hier: viel übrig haben für **habit** ['hæbɪt] (An)Gewohnheit **keep odd hours** [ɒd 'aʊəz] keine festen Zeiten einhalten **study** ['stʌdɪ] Arbeitszimmer **mongrel pup** ['mʌŋgrəl pʌp] junger Bastardhund **distemper** [dɪs'tempə] Staupe **dog-licence** ['dɒglaɪsəns] Erlaubnisschein zum Halten e-s Hundes **none the less** nichtsdestoweniger

For another moment he stared at the window as if he **cordially disliked** it; then he stepped suddenly from the kerb and went **briskly** across the road.

*

Nor was I far behind him. Mine is on the whole a dull and **uneventful** existence, and I was in no hurry to **seek** my bed. If the open window of Mr. Thrall looked a bit queer to the policeman, it looked no less queer to me, and I was **resolved** that the law should have my company until he drove me away with **oaths**. Life is not so **gay** nowadays that one can **afford** to ignore even the **vaguest** promise of entertainment. Besides, every **Holmes** must have his **Watson**, and it would be nice, I felt, for the policeman to have me at his side to **gape** at his **deductions**. So I went after him at a high speed, and **caught him up** as he set his hand on Mr.Thrall's neat little iron gate.

'If it's a burglar,' I said respectfully, 'I can hold your coat. If it's two burglars, I can run for help. If it's several burglars, I can take any messages to your **next of kin**.'

But the policeman answered never a word, nor did he **by so much as a glance acknowledge** my presence. Through the gate he went and with a **firm** and **purposeful** step across

---

cordially dislike s.th. ['kɔːdjəlɪ dɪs'laɪk] et. gründlich verabscheuen **brisk** [brɪsk] rasch u. energisch **uneventful** ['ʌnɪ'ventfʊl] ereignislos, ruhig **seek** [siːk] aufsuchen **resolved** [rɪ'zɒlvd] fest entschlossen **oath** [əʊθ] Fluch, Verwünschung **gay** [geɪ] lustig **afford** [ə'fɔːd] sich leisten od. erlauben **vaguest** ['veɪgɪst] Superlativ von **vague** [veɪg] vage, unbestimmt **Holmes, Watson = Sherlock Holmes, Dr. Watson** ['ʃɜːlɒk həʊmz, 'wɒtsn] aus Sir Arthur Conan Doyles Sherlock-Holmes-Geschichten **gape** [geɪp] den Mund aufreißen (vor Erstaunen) **deduction** [dɪ'dʌkʃn] Schlussfolgerung **caught him up** [kɔːt] von **catch s.o. up** j-n einholen **next of kin** [nekst, kɪn] nächste Verwandte (auch Pl) **(never) by so much as a glance** [glɑːns] nicht einmal mit e-m Blick **acknowledge** [ək'nɒlɪdʒ] zur Kenntnis nehmen **firm** [fɜːm] fest, sicher **purposeful** ['pɜːpəsfʊl] zielbewusst, entschlossen

the neat little **patch of grass** that lay between the house and the road. Arrived at the open window, he stopped, leaned forward across the **sill**, pulled aside a curtain and **peered** in. I **ranged myself beside** him and did **likewise**, but the room beyond was dark, and I could make out nothing of any interest.

'Unpleasant furniture, isn't it?' I said. 'I always think an **antimacassar** is a sign of an **ingrowing** mind. I have an aunt who —'

'*Ah!*' said the policeman, so sharply and so suddenly that I jumped. And with that he stepped back a **pace**, swung his long legs over the sill and dropped into the room. All this without a word to me, which **irked** me somewhat; for if my personality—as some say—is unimpressive, I like to think that there is at least a something about me that **commands** attention. However, it is never my way to quarrel with policemen, so I said no more about my aunt, but in my turn threw a leg across the sill and stood within the room.

Of that room which was the study of Mr. Alaric Thrall I have very little to say, and nothing **complimentary**. It was just such a room as one would expect the study of Mr. Alaric Thrall to be. A large and airless and **faintly sinister** room, most unhappily **appointed**. There was a red **wallpaper** that hurt the eye, a red plush sofa that **was a weariness to see**,

---

patch of grass [pætʃ, grɑːs] Rasenstück **sill** [sɪl] = **window-sill** Fensterbrett **peer** [pɪə] spähen **range o.s. beside s.o.** [reɪndʒ, bɪˈsaɪd] sich neben j-n stellen **likewise** [ˈlaɪkwaɪz] ebenfalls **antimacassar** [ˈæntɪməˈkæsə] Sofaschoner **ingrowing** [ˈɪngrəʊɪŋ] nach innen gewandt, sich abschließend **pace** [peɪs] Schritt **irk** [ɜːk] ärgern **command** [kəˈmɑːnd] verdienen **complimentary** [kɒmplɪˈmentərɪ] schmeichelhaft **faintly** [ˈfeɪntlɪ] schwach, hier: etwas, ein bisschen **sinister** [ˈsɪnɪstə] unheimlich **appointed** [əˈpɔɪntɪd] eingerichtet, ausgestattet **wallpaper** [ˈwɔːlpeɪpə] Tapete **that was a weariness to see** [ˈwɪərɪnɪs] hier: langweilig aussehend and four **gilt-framed** pictures of the kind that grocers, there being no law against it, are **apt to inflict** at Christmas **upon** their more profitable **customers**. Also a leather armchair, a **revolving** bookcase and a wide desk whereon lay many papers **in confusion**. The atmosphere **suggested** that whoever had opened the window had followed no known **precedent**.

The policeman was standing by the desk, his back to me; and as I came through the window he whipped about, saying with extraordinary rapidity and emphasis:

'Stay where you are! Don't touch a thing!'

It was then that, for the first time in my life, I **defied** a policeman; for I did not stay where I was. Had I stayed, I could not have seen the thing that lay upon the floor beyond the desk—the thing whose **outflung** hand had caught my eye as I came in over the windowsill. Wishing to see that thing, I defied the policeman and **unobtrusively** moved sideways until I had **achieved my object**.

That which lay upon the floor was, or had been, a man; an elderly man, grey-haired and of a **portly habit**, though tall and strongly made. He was **clad** in pyjamas and a dressing-gown, and he lay upon his back with his arms thrown out and his head **twisted** to one side in an unnatural way. His face was turned to the ceiling, and it was not a pleasant face to look upon at half past four of a bright June morning. In-

---

gilt-framed ['gɪltfreɪmd] mit Goldrahmen **be apt** [æpt] neigen, hier: pflegen **inflict upon s.o.** [ɪn'flɪkt] j-m aufdrängen **customers** Pl ['kʌstəməz] Kunden Pl, Kundschaft **revolving** [rɪ'vɒlvɪŋ] drehbar **in confusion** [kən'fjuːʒn] heillos durcheinander **suggest** hindeuten od. schließen lassen auf **precedent** ['presɪdənt] Präzedenzfall, Beispiel **whip about = whip round** [wɪp] sich ruckartig umdrehen **defy** [dɪ'faɪ] die Stirn bieten, sich widersetzen **outflung** ['aʊt'flʌŋ] ausgebreitet, hier: ausgestreckt **unobtrusive** ['ʌnəb'truːsɪv] unauffällig **achieve one's object** [ə'tʃiːv, 'ɒbdʒɪkt] sein Ziel erreichen **portly** ['pɔːtlɪ] wohlbeleibt **habit** Konstitution, körperliche Verfassung **clad** [klæd] gekleidet **twist** [twɪst] drehen

deed, it had never been a pleasant face to look upon at any time, so **legibly** was evil **stamped** upon its every **feature**: the cold, narrow eyes, the **predatory nose**, the thin, cruel, **sneering** mouth. This had been an unloved and unlovable man, and was now a very dead man indeed.

Said the policeman, standing by the desk and looking down upon what remained of this man:

'Your Mr. Thrall—eh?'

'Yes,' I said. 'How—?'

'Broken neck,' said the policeman, adding **as it were** to himself: 'Somebody broke it for him not very long ago.'

At this I drew a long breath and leant upon the high back of the leather chair.

'Then somebody,' I said, 'has done the world **a very good turn** indeed. There are quite a lot of people who won't weep to hear of this.'

'You think so?' said the policeman.

'That,' said I, nodding at the thing upon the floor, was a bad man, officer, if ever there was one. The ***de mortuis*** business doesn't **apply** in his case, because there's nothing good you can say of him, you see. A real bad man, he was.'

'As bad as that?' said the policeman.

'Worse than that,' said I. 'A **money-lender by trade** and a **blackmailer** in his **spare time**. **At a guess** I'd say there are at

---

legible ['ledʒəbl] deutlich **stamp upon** [stæmp] aufprägen auf **feature** ['fiːtʃə] (Gesichts)Zug **predatory nose** ['predətərɪ nəʊz] Raubvogelnase **sneering** ['snɪərɪŋ] höhnisch grinsend **as it were** sozusagen, gleichsam **has done the world a good turn** j-m e-n guten Dienst erweisen **the de mortuis business** ['deɪ 'mɔːtjʊɪs 'bɪznɪs] das „von den Toten soll man nur Gutes sagen" Zeug **apply** [ə'plaɪ] zutreffen **money-lender** ['mʌnɪlendə] Geldverleiher **by trade** [treɪd] von Beruf **blackmailer** ['blækmeɪlə] Erpresser **spare time** [speə taɪm] Freizeit **at a guess** [ges] bei bloßer Schätzung

least fifty people who'd have loved to break his neck and **take the consequences**.'

'Well, one of them has done it,' said the policeman, and again he looked at me. 'You seem,' he said, for the second time in ten minutes, 'to know a good deal about him.'

'I do,' said I. 'Because I know a **fellow** who once **had dealings with** this—gentleman.'

'Ah?' said the policeman.

'The fellow,' I said, '**dropped** a **pot of money—racing**—and he came to Mr. Thrall for a **loan**. He got it, and he got his lesson, too. Because when he'd paid back about twice as much as he'd originally borrowed, he found there was still a good bit **owing**, and he couldn't **raise** it anywhere. So he came to Mr. Thrall and asked for a little more time, and Mr. Thrall said he was sorry, but he needed the money at once, and couldn't the fellow—ah—borrow the necessary from his firm and—ah—pay it back later? You see the idea?'

'And what happened?' asked the policeman, staring down at the thing at his feet.

But at this point it **occured to** me that we were hardly **exhibiting** that initiative and **resource** which the Law expects of those who discover dead bodies in the small hours of a bright June morning.

---

take the consequences ['kɒnsɪkwənsɪz] die Folgen tragen **fellow** ['feləʊ] Bursche, Mensch **have dealings with s.o.** ['diːlɪŋz] mit j-m zu tun haben **drop** sl. [drɒp] verlieren, loswerden **a pot of money** sl. ein Heidengeld **racing** ['reɪsɪŋ] (Pferde)Rennsport; Rennen **loan** [ləʊn] Darlehen, Kredit **be owing** ['əʊɪŋ] zu zahlen sein, noch offen stehen **raise** [reɪz] beschaffen (Geld) **occur to s.o.** [ə'kɜː] j-m einfallen **exhibit** [ɪg'zɪbɪt] zeigen, entfalten **resource** [rɪ'sɔːs] Findigkeit, Wendigkeit

'Don't you think,' I suggested **diffidently**, 'we ought to take steps of some sort? What about a doctor, for one thing?'

The policeman **started** and looked **swiftly** about the room.

'Telephone?' he demanded **curtly**.

'In the hall,' said I.

'Stay where you are,' said the policeman as he went out.

*

In the fullness of time there was an **inquest**. And at this inquest many interesting facts concerning the late Mr. Thrall were **dragged** into the light of day, so that no single voice was heard to express regret at his **passing**. Indeed, a dead Mr. Thrall was shown to be so **infinitely preferable** to a live one that the absence of any **clue** whatsoever to the identity of his **executioner** was generally held to be a **cause** for satisfaction. The policeman (whose name—rather disappointingly, I felt—**proved** to be Jones) and I having **severally** described our small part in the affair, and such other **evidence** as was available having been given and debated, the **jury** had no **hesitation** in **concluding** that Mr. Alaric Thrall had met his death at the hands of some person or person unknown. The **foreman**'s manner of announcing this decision **implied**

---

diffident ['dɪfɪdənt] schüchtern **start** [stɑːt] zusammenfahren, -zucken **swift** [swɪft] schnell, rasch **curt** [kɜːt] barsch, schroff **in the fullness of time** ['fʊlnɪs] zu gegebener Zeit **inquest** ['ɪnkwest] gerichtliche Verhandlung zur Feststellung der Todesursache (bei ungeklärten Todesfällen) **drag** [dræg] zerren **passing** ['pɑːsɪŋ] Ableben, Hinscheiden **infinite** ['ɪnfɪnɪt] unendlich **preferable to s.o.** ['prefərəbl] j-m vorzuziehen **clue** [kluː] Spur, Anhaltspunkt **executioner** [eksɪ'kjuːʃnə] Henker **cause for** [kɔːz] Grund od. Anlass zu **prove to be** [pruːv] sich herausstellen als **severally** ['sevrəlɪ] jeder für sich **evidence having been given** ['evɪdəns] von **give evidence** e-e Aussage machen **jury** ['dʒʊərɪ] (die) Geschworenen **have no hesitation** [hezɪ'teɪʃn] keinen Augenblick zögern **conclude** [kən'kluːd] beschließen, entscheiden **foreman** ['fɔːmən] Sprecher (der Geschworenen) **imply** [ɪm'plaɪ] durchblicken lassen

that, in the jury's opinion, the matter might very well **be left at that**. Which—as there was nothing more that could be done—it was.

Now it came about that some three weeks after the conclusion of these **proceedings** I was bidden to dine with a Mrs. Wymondham, who lives in Hyde Park Place. This invitation I accepted **with alacrity**, for Mrs. Wymondham happens also to be my cousin Jane, and what she does not know about the art of giving dinners has not yet been discovered or invented. To Hyde Park Place, therefore, I went **on eager feet**; and when I had been led to the drawing-room, **endowed** with sherry and congratulated upon my **association** with one of the best murders of the year, I led my cousin Jane aside and said to her:

'I'm thinking of starting on my reminiscences, so show me all the **nibs**.'

'I'm afraid,' said my cousin Jane, 'they're a **stuffy lot** tonight—mostly political. Let me see—old Blake you know, and Mrs. Coopington, and Sir Charles and the Wentwort twins. Oh, and there's Mrs. Clinton-Duke—you've not met her, I think.'

'Do you advise it?' said I.

'Oh, you'll like her,' said my cousin Jane. 'She's a dear and she's had a very rough time of it. A little while ago she had

---

be left at that von **leave it at that** es dabei bewenden lassen **proceedings** Pl [prə'siːdɪŋz] Vorgänge, Vorfälle **with alacrity** [ə'lækrɪtɪ] bereitwillig(st) **on eager feet** auf ungeduldigen Füßen **endow** [ɪn'daʊ] ausstatten **association** [əsəʊsɪ'eɪʃn] Verbindung, Beziehung **nibs** F [nɪbz] großes Tier **stuffy** F ['stʌfɪ] spießig, verknöchert, steif **lot** F [lɒt] Gesellschaft

some awful trouble over money—I don't quite know what—and she was the unhappiest thing on earth. But her son—he's here, too—came home from America and **straightened** it **out** for her, and she's all right again now. Come along.'

Thereupon she took me by the arm and **conducted** me to a far corner, where sat an elderly and white-haired lady whose face bore unmistakable **traces** of that unhappiness of which my cousin Jane had spoken. But that Mrs. Clinton-Duke was not unhappy now was very **evident** from the smile with which she greeted me and the manner in which she turned to the young man who stood—all **cuffs** and shirt-front—in the shadow behind her, bidding him come forth and make my acquaintance.

Obediently young Mr. Clinton-Duke **emerged** from the background, holding out his hand. I shook it, but in a **dazed** and feeble way, for I was immeasurably astonished. For this Clinton-Duke was a very high, very broad, very efficient-looking young man, with keen blue eyes and very red hair and a chin like the toe of a football boot. So I **goggled at** him, and he **frowned at** me ever so slightly, spoke briefly to his mother and politely but **irresistibly shepherded** me away.

When we were **out of earshot**:

'You'll **oblige me**,' said he tranquilly, 'by not mentioning

---

straighten out ['streɪtn] in Ordnung bringen **conduct** [kən'dʌkt] führen, geleiten **trace** [treɪs] Spur, (An)Zeichen **evident** ['evɪdənt] offensichtlich, hier: deutlich zu sehen **cuff** [kʌf] Manschette **obedient** [ə'biːdjənt] gehorsam **emerge** [ɪ'mɜːdʒ] hervorkommen **dazed** [deɪzd] betäubt, verwirrt **goggle at s.o.** ['gɒgl] j-n anglotzen **frown at s.o.** [fraʊn] j-n stirnrunzelnd ansehen **irresistible** [ɪrɪ'zɪstəbl] unwiderstehlich **shepherd away** ['ʃepəd] fortführen, F wegbugsieren **out of earshot** ['ɪəʃɒt] außer Hörweite **you will oblige me ... by not mentioning** [ə'blaɪdʒ, 'menʃnɪŋ] seien Sie so freundlich und erwähnen Sie nicht ...

that—affair to her. She doesn't know I was mixed up in it—different name, you see—and I don't want her to know.'

'All right,' said I. 'But—'

'Good show by Kent yesterday,' said Clinton-Duke. 'I'll bet the **bowlers** are **cursing** this weather. Well, if you'll excuse me, I ought to be—'

'Half a second,' said I. And I **thrust** a hand into my pocket and brought out a small, **gleaming** object which I offered to him upon my **palm**. 'This is yours, I think.'

The face of Clinton-Duke became suddenly hard and **blank**, and as empty of all expression as the face of a wooden idol. For a long moment he said no word, but stood staring **fixedly** at the thing in my hand. A button it was—a small, shining, silverish button such as policemen wear down in front of them.

'Where,' said Clinton-Duke, in a very gentle voice, 'did you find that?'

'On the floor under his hand,' said I, 'while you were telephoning in the hall. I kept it because I didn't understand how you came to lose it. But now I think I do.'

'Yes?' said Clinton-Duke.

'I may be wrong,' I said, 'but this is how it looks to me. Suppose, now, that I was a policeman and I wanted to **abolish** a **bloke** who lived on my beat. I think I'd **knock him up**

---

bowler ['bəʊlə] Bowler (Kricket: der Werfer der Schlagpartei, der auf das gegnerische Tor = Wicket wirft) **curse** [kɜːs] verfluchen, fluchen auf **thrust** [θrʌst] stecken, schieben **gleaming** ['gliːmɪŋ] glänzend **palm** [pɑːm] Handfläche, hohle Hand **blank** [blæŋk] ausdruckslos **fixed** [fɪkst] unverwandt **abolish** [ə'bɒlɪʃ] vernichten **bloke** sl. [bləʊk] Kerl, Bursche **knock up** [nɒk] wecken (durch Klopfen), herausklopfen

on some excuse in the very early hours, **blot** him **out**, leave the window open, get back on my beat and wait. Then **presently** some innocent **boob** would come along, **all flushed with** wine, and I'd draw his attention to the window and **trot off** to **investigate**. The boob, naturally, would come along too, and together we'd discover the body. It would be a kind of alibi, don't you see? And it would be **dashed rough luck** if I lost a button on my first visit, and the boob happened to **spot** it and wonder how it got there.'

There followed a little pause, while Clinton-Duke looked at me as if he were seeing me for the first time. And then, quite suddenly:

'You're right,' he said, 'except that I didn't mean to blot him out. He'd been blackmailing my mother, you see. He had some letters. ... But she didn't tell me till he'd taken her last cent and was asking for more. She was ill with worry, so I **chucked** my job in New York and came home. I went to see Thrall, but he laughed at me and **turned me out**. Then I joined the police, because I had no money, and I had to get work till I'd decided what to do. It was just luck that I was sent to that **division**. That morning Thrall came home about an hour before you **showed up**. He didn't notice me, and I let him go in. Then I thought it would be a good chance to **have it out with him**, so I knocked him up. I didn't mean to

---

blot out [blɒt] auslöschen, vernichten **presently** ['prezntlɪ] bald darauf, alsbald **boob** [buːb] Trottel, Einfaltspinsel **all flushed with wine** [flʌʃt, waɪn] voll des süßen Weines **trot off** F [trɒt] ab-, losziehen **investigate** [ɪn'vestɪgeɪt] Nachforschungen anstellen; untersuchen **dashed** F [dæʃt] verflucht, -flixt **rough luck** [lʌk] Pech **spot** [spɒt] entdecken, erspähen **chuck (up)** F [tʃʌk] aufgeben **turn out** hinauswerfen **division** [dɪ'vɪʒn] Bezirk **show up** F auftauchen, -kreuzen **have it out with s.o.** die Sache mit j-m endgültig bereinigen

hurt him, but he **turned nasty** and the next thing I knew his neck was broken. Then I took the letters and came away. ... My mother thinks he **repented** and sent me the letters before he died.'

'And you're not a policeman now?' I said.

'No,' said Clinton-Duke. 'I got a better job a week ago.' He paused again, considering me. 'Well,' he said calmly, 'what are you going to do about it?'

'You remember,' said I, 'my telling you about a fellow I know who borrowed money from Thrall?'

'Ah!' said Clinton-Duke. 'I thought so, somehow.'

'If Thrall hadn't died when he did,' I said, 'the chances are that I'd have done what he suggested—stolen from the firm to pay him back. ... Personally, I don't think so much of Kent's **batting** this year. Anybody could make **runs** on the kind of **wickets** we've been having lately.'

---

turn werden **nasty** ['nɑːstɪ] gemein, niederträchtig, boshaft **repent** [rɪ'pent] bereuen **batting** ['bætɪŋ] Schlagen, Schläge Pl (Kricket) **run** [rʌn] Lauf (Kricket) **wicket** ['wɪkɪt] Wicket, Dreistab, Tor (Kricket)

The Fountain Plays

By *Dorothy L. Sayers*

'Yes,' said Mr. Spiller, in a satisfied tone, 'I must say I like a bit of **ornamental** water. Gives a **finish** to the place.

'The Versailles **touch**,' agreed Ronald Proudfoot.

Mr. Spiller glanced sharply at him, as though **suspecting** sarcasm, but his **lean** face expressed nothing whatever. Mr. Spiller was never quite **at his ease** in the company of his daughter's **fiancé**, though he was proud of the girl's **achievement**. With all his (to Mr. Spiller) **unamiable** qualities, Ronald Proudfoot was a perfect gentleman, and Betty was completely **wrapped up in** him.

'The only thing it wants,' continued Mr. Spiller, 'to *my* mind, that is, is **Opening Up**. To make a **Vista**, so to say. You don't get the Effect with these bushes on all four sides.'

'Oh, I don't know, Mr. Spiller,' **objected** Mrs. Digby in her mild voice. 'Don't you think it makes rather a fascinating surprise? You come along the path, never dreaming there's anything behind those **lilacs**, and then you turn the corner and come suddenly upon it. I'm sure, when you brought me down to see it this afternoon, it quite took my breath away.'

'There's that, of course,' admitted Mr. Spiller. It **occurred**

---

fountain ['faʊntɪn] Springbrunnen **play** [pleɪ] in Betrieb sein **ornamental water** [ɔːnə'mentl] Ziergewässer **finish** ['fɪnɪʃ] letzter Schliff **touch** [tʌtʃ] (besondere) Note **suspect** [səs'pekt] argwöhnen **lean** [liːn] hager, mager **at one's ease** [iːz] gelöst **fiancé** [fiɑ̃'ːŋseɪ] Verlobte(r) **achievement** [ə'tʃiːvmənt] Errungenschaft **unamiable** [ʌn'eɪmjəbl] unliebenswürdig **be wrapped up in** [ræpt] ganz aufgehen in **opening up** hier: e-e Öffnung zu schaffen **vista** ['vɪstə] Ausblick **object** [əb'dʒekt] einwenden **lilac** ['laɪlək] Flieder; Pl Fliederbüsche **it occurred to him** [ə'kɜːd] es kam ihm der Gedanke

to him not for the first time, that there was something very attractive about Mrs. Digby's **silvery** personality. She had **distinction**, too. A widow and widower of the **sensible** time of life, with a bit of money on both sides, might do worse than settle down comfortably in a pleasant house with half an acre of garden and a bit of ornamental water.

'And it's so pretty and **secluded**,' went on Mrs. Digby, 'with these **glorious** rhododendrons. Look how pretty they are, all **sprayed** with the water—like **fairy** jewels—and the **rustic** seat against those dark cypresses at the back. Really Italian. And the **scent** of the lilac is so marvellous!'

Mr. Spiller knew that the cypresses were, in fact, **yews**, but he did not correct her. A little ignorance was **becoming** in a woman. He glanced from the **cotoneasters** at one side of the fountain to the rododendrons on the other, their rainbow **flower-trusses** sparkling with diamond drops.

'I wasn't thinking of touching the rhododendrons or the cotoneasters,' he said. 'I only thought of cutting through that great hedge of lilac, so as to make a vista from the house. But the ladies must always have the last word, mustn't they—er—Ronald?' (He never could bring out Proudfoot's Christian name naturally). 'If you like it as it is, Mrs. Digby, that settles it. The lilacs shall stay.'

'It's too **flattering** of you,' said Mrs. Digby, 'but you must-

---

silvery ['sɪlvərɪ] strahlend, glänzend **distinction** [dɪs'tɪŋkʃn] Vornehmheit, Würde **sensible** ['sensəbl] vernünftig **secluded** [sɪ'klu:dɪd] einsam, abgelegen **glorious** ['glɔ:rɪəs] herrlich **sprayed** [spreɪd] besprüht, bespritzt **fairy** ['feərɪ] zart, fein **rustic** ['rʌstɪk] einfach, schlicht, roh gearbeitet **scent** [sent] Duft, Geruch **yew** [ju:] Eibe **becoming** [bɪ'kʌmɪŋ] gut stehen **cotoneaster** [kətəʊnɪ'æstə] Steinmispel **flower-truss** ['flaʊətrʌs] Blütendolde **flattering** ['flætərɪŋ] schmeichelhaft

n't think of **altering** your plans for me. I haven't any right to **interfere with** your beautiful garden.'

'Indeed you have,' said Mr. Spiller. 'I **defer to** your taste entirely. You have spoken for the lilacs, and **henceforward** they are **sacred**.'

'I shall be afraid to give an opinion on anything, after that,' said Mrs. Digby, shaking her head. 'But whatever you decide to do, I'm sure it will be lovely. It was a marvellous idea to think of putting the fountain there. It makes all the difference to the garden.'

Mr. Spiller thought she was quite right. And indeed, though the fountain was rather flattered by the name of 'ornamental water', consisting as it did of a **marble basin** set in the centre of a **pool** about four feet **square**, it made a brave show, with its **plume** of dancing water, fifteen feet high, **towering over** the smaller **shrubs** and almost overtopping the tall lilacs. And its cooling splash and tinkle **soothed** the ear on this pleasant day of early summer.

'Costs a bit to run, doesn't it?' demanded Mr. Gooch. He had been silent up till now, and Mrs. Digby felt that his remark **betrayed** a rather **sordid** outlook on life. Indeed, from the first moment of meeting Mr. Gooch, she had **pronounced** him **decidedly** common, and wondered that he should be **on such intimate terms** with her **host**.

---

alter ['ɔːltə] ändern **interfere with** [ɪntə'fɪə] sich einmischen in **defer to** [dɪ'fɜː] sich fügen **henceforward** ['hens'fɔːwəd] von nun an **sacred** ['seɪkrɪd] heilig **marble basin** ['mɑːbl 'beɪsn] Marmorbecken **pool** [puːl] Bassin **square** [skweə] im Quadrat **plume of ... water** [pluːm, 'wɔːtə] hier: Wasserstrahl **tower over** ['taʊə] überragen **shrub** [ʃrʌb] Strauch, Busch **soothe** [suːð] beruhigen(d wirken auf) **betray** [bɪ'treɪ] verraten **sordid** ['sɔːdɪd] niedrig, schäbig **pronounce** [prə'naʊns] bezeichnen als **decidedly** [dɪ'saɪdɪdlɪ] zweifellos, offensichtlich **on intimate terms** ['ɪntɪmɪt tɜːmz] auf vertrautem Fuß **host** [həʊst] Gastgeber, Hausherr

'No, no,' replied Mr. Spiller. 'No, it's not expensive. You see, it uses the same water over and over again. Most **ingenious**. The fountains in Trafalgar Square work on the same principle, I believe. Of course, I had to pay a bit to have it put in, but I think it's worth the money.'

'Yes, indeed,' said Mrs. Digby.

'I always said you were a **warm** man, Spiller,' said Mr. Gooch, with his vulgar laugh. 'Wish I was in your shoes. A **snug** spot, that's what I call this place. Snug.'

'I'm not a millionaire,' answered Mr. Spiller, rather shortly. 'But things might be worse in these times. Of course,' he added, more cheerfully, 'one has to be careful. I turn the fountain off at night, for instance, to save **leakage** and **waste**.'

'I'll swear you do, you damned old **miser**,' said Mr. Gooch, **offensively**.

Mr. Spiller was saved replying by the sounding of a gong in the distance.

'Ah! there's dinner,' he announced, with a certain **relief** in his tone. The party wound their way out between the lilacs, and **paced** gently up the long **crazy** pavement, past the **herbaceous borders** and the two long beds of **raw** little **ticketed** roses, to the glorified villa which Mr. Spiller had **christened** 'The **Pleasaunce**'.

---

ingenious [ɪn'dʒiːnjəs] genial, klug **warm** BE [wɔːm] wohlhabend **snug** [snʌg] behaglich u. geborgen **leakage** ['liːkɪdʒ] Lecken, Auslaufen **waste** [weɪst] Verschwendung **miser** ['maɪzə] Geizhals **offensive** [ə'fensɪv] beleidigend **relief** [rɪ'liːf] Erleichterung **pace** [peɪs] schreiten **crazy** ['kreɪzɪ] unregelmäßig **herbaceous border** [hɜː'beɪʃəs 'bɔːdə] (Stauden)Rabatte **raw** [rɔː] ganz neu **ticketed** ['tɪkɪtɪd] etikettiert **christen** ['krɪsn] taufen **pleasa(u)nce** ['plezəns] Lustgarten, hier: Lustschloss

It seemed to Mrs. Digby that there was a slightly **strained** atosphere about dinner, though Betty, pretty as a picture and very much in love with Ronald Proudfoot, made a perfectly charming little hostess. The **jarring note** was sounded by Mr. Gooch. He ate too noisily, drank far too freely, got on Proudfoot's nerves and behaved to Mr. Spiller with a kind of **veiled insolence** which was embarrassing and disagreeable to listen to. She wondered again where he had come from, and why Mr. Spiller **put up with** him. She knew little about him, except that from time to time he turned up on a visit to 'The Pleasaunce,' usually staying there about a month and being, apparently, well **supplied** with cash. She had an idea that he was some kind of **commission agent**, though she could not recall any **distinct** statement on this point. Mr. Spiller had settled down in the village about three years **previously**, and she had always liked him. Though not, in any sense of the word, a cultivated man, he was kind, generous and **unassuming**, and his **devotion** to Betty had something very lovable about it. Mr. Gooch had started coming about a year later. Mrs. Digby said to herself that if ever she was in a position to **lay down the law** at 'The Pleasaunce'—and she had begun to think matters were tending that way—her influence would be directed to getting rid of Mr. Gooch.

'How about a spot of bridge?' suggested Ronald Proudfoot,

---

strained [streɪnd] gespannt **jarring note** ['dʒɑːrɪŋ nəʊt] Misston **veiled** [veɪld] verschleiert, versteckt **insolence** ['ɪnsələns] Unverschämtheit **put up with s.o.** sich et. von j-m gefallen lassen **supplied** [sə'plaɪd] versorgt **commission agent** [kə'mɪʃn 'eɪdʒənt] Provisionsvertreter **distinct** [dɪs'tɪŋkt] klar, deutlich **previously** ['priːvjəslɪ] zuvor **unassuming** ['ʌnə'sjuːmɪŋ] anspruchslos, bescheiden **devotion** [dɪ'vəʊʃn] Zuneigung, Liebe **lay down the law** (alles) bestimmen, den Ton angeben

when coffee had been served. It was nice, reflected Mrs. Digby, to have coffee brought in by the **manservant**. Masters was really a very well-trained butler, though he did combine the office with that of chauffeur. One would be comfortable at 'The Pleasaunce'. From the dining-room window she could see the **neat** garage housing the **Wolseley saloon** on the ground floor, with a room for the chauffeur above it, and **topped off** by a handsome **gilded weather-vane aglitter** in the last rays of the sun. A good cook, a **smart parlourmaid** and everything done exactly as one could wish—if she were to marry Mr. Spiller she would be able, for the first time in her life, to afford a personal maid as well. There would be plenty of room in the house, and of course, when Betty was married—

Betty, she thought, was not overpleased that Ronald had suggested bridge. Bridge is not a game that lends itself to the expression of tender feeling, and it would perhaps have looked better if Ronald had **enticed** Betty out to sit in the lilac scented **dusk** under the yew-hedge by the fountain. Mrs. Digby was sometimes afraid that Betty was the more in love of the two. But if Ronald wanted anything he had to have it, of course, and personally, Mrs. Digby enjoyed nothing better than a quiet **rubber**. Besides, the arrangement had the advantage that it got rid of Mr. Gooch. 'Don't play bridge,' Mr.

---

manservant ['mænsɜːvənt] Diener **neat** [niːt] sauber, gepflegt **Wolseley** ['wʊlzlɪ] englische Automarke **saloon** BE [sə'luːn] Limousine **topped off** [tɒpt] gekrönt **gilded** ['gɪldɪd] vergoldet, golden **weather-vane** ['weðəveɪn] Wetterfahne **aglitter** [ə'glɪtə] glitzernd, strahlend **smart** [smɑːt] adrett; geschickt **parlourmaid** ['pɑːləmeɪd] Haus-, Stubenmädchen **entice** [ɪn'taɪs] verleiten **dusk** [dʌsk] Abenddämmerung **rubber** ['rʌbə] Robber (Doppel- od. Dreierpartie im Whist- od. Bridgespiel)

Gooch **was wont** to say. 'Never had time to learn. We didn't play bridge where I was brought up.' He repeated the remark now, and followed it up with a **contemptuous snort** directed at Mr. Spiller.

'Never too late to begin,' said the latter **pacifically**.

'Not me!' **retorted** Mr. Gooch, 'I'm going to have a turn in the garden. Where's that fellow Masters? Tell him to take the whisky and soda down to the fountain. The **decanter**, mind—one drink's no good to **yours truly**.' He **plunged** a thick hand into the box of **Coronas** on the side-table, took out a handful of cigars and passed out through the **French window** of the library on to the terrace. Mr. Spiller rang the bell and gave the order without comment, and **presently** they saw Masters **pad** down the long crazy path between the rose-beds and the herbaceous borders, baring the whisky and soda on a tray.

The other four played on till 10.30, when, a rubber coming to an end, Mrs. Digby rose and said it was time she went home. Her host gallantly offered to accompany her. 'These two young people can look after themselves for a moment,' he added, with a **conspiratorial** smile.

'The young can look after themselves better than the old, these days.' She laughed a little shyly, and raised no objection when Mr. Spiller drew her hand into his arm as they

---

be wont to say [wəʊnt] zu sagen pflegen **contemptuous** [kən'temptjʊəs] verächtlich, geringschätzig **snort** [snɔːt] Schnauben **pacific** [pə'sɪfɪk] friedfertig **retort** [rɪ'tɔːt] erwidern, entgegnen **decanter** [dɪ'kæntə] Karaffe **yours truly** F meine Wenigkeit **plunge** [plʌndʒ] tauchen, (ver)graben **Coronas** [kə'rəʊnəs] e-e Zigarrenmarke **French window** Terrassen-, Balkontür **presently** ['prezntlɪ] gleich od. bald darauf **pad** [pæd] trotten **conspiratorial** [kənspɪrə'tɔːrɪəl] verschwörerisch

walked the couple of hundred yards to her cottage. She hesitated a moment whether to ask him in, but decided that a sweet **decorum suited** her style best. She stretched out a soft, beringed hand to him over the top of the little white gate. His **pressure lingered**—he would have kissed the hand, so **insidious** was the scent of the red and white **hawthorns** in her **trim** garden, but before he had **summoned up courage**, she had withdrawn it from his **clasp** and was gone.

Mr. Spiller, opening his own front door in an agreeable dream, **encountered** Masters.

'Where is everybody, Masters?'

'Mr. Proudfoot left five or ten minutes since, sir, and Miss Elizabeth has **retired**.'

'Oh!' Mr. Spiller was a little **startled**. The new generation, he thought sadly, did not make love like the old. He hoped there was nothing wrong. Another irritating thought presented itself.

'Has Mr. Gooch come in?'

'I could not say, sir. Shall I go and see?'

'No, never mind.' If Gooch had been **sozzling himself up** with whisky since dinner-time, it was just as well Masters should keep away from him. You never knew. Masters was one of these soft-spoken **beggars**, but he might take advantage. Better not to trust servants, anyhow.

---

decorum [dɪ'kɔːrəm] Etikette, Anstand **suit** [sjuːt] passen zu **pressure** ['preʃə] hier: Händedruck **linger** ['lɪŋgə] verweilen **insidous** [ɪn'sɪdɪəs] tückisch, hier: verlockend u. gefährlich **red (white) hawthorn** ['hɔːθɔːn] Rot(Weiß)dorn **trim** [trɪm] schmuck, hübsch, sauber **summon up courage** ['sʌmən, 'kʌrɪdʒ] s-n Mut zusammennehmen **clasp** [klɑːsp] Umklammerung **encounter** [ɪn'kaʊntə] begegnen **retire** [rɪ'taɪə] sich zur Ruhe begeben **startled** ['stɑːtld] bestürzt, überrascht **sozzle o.s. up** sl. ['sɒzl] sich völlig besaufen **beggar** F ['begə] Bursche, Kerl

'You can cut along to bed. I'll lock up.'

'Very good, sir.'

'Oh, by the way, is the fountain turned off?'

'Yes, sir. I turned it off myself, sir, at half past ten, seeing that you were engaged, sir.'

'Quite right. Good night, Masters.'

'Good night, sir.'

He heard the man go out by the back and cross the paved **court** to the garage. Thoughtfully he **bolted** both entrances, and returned to the library. The whisky decanter was not in its usual place—no doubt it was still with Gooch in the garden—but he mixed himself a small brandy and soda, and drank it. He supposed he must now face the **tiresome** business of getting Gooch up to bed. Then, suddenly, he realized that the encounter would take place here and not in the garden. Gooch was coming in through the French window. He was drunk, **but not**, Mr. Spiller observed with relief, **incapably so**.

'Well?' said Gooch.

'Well?' retorted Mr. Spiller.

'Had a good time with the **accommodating** widow, eh? Enjoyed yourself? Lucky old **hound**, aren't you? **Fallen soft** in your old age, eh?'

'There, that'll do,' said Mr. Spiller.

---

court [kɔːt] Hof **bolt** [bəʊlt] verriegeln **tiresome** ['taɪəsəm] lästig **but not incapably so** [ɪn'keɪpəblɪ] aber nicht so, dass er zu nichts mehr fähig war **accommodating** [ə'kɒmədeɪtɪŋ] gefällig, entgegenkommend **hound** sl. [haʊnd] Schurke, Hund **fallen soft** ['fɔːlən] von **fall soft** gefühlvoll werden

'Oh, will it? That's good. That's **rich**. That'll do, eh? Think I'm Masters, talking to me like that?' Mr. Gooch gave a thick **chuckle**. 'Well, I'm not Masters, I'm master here. Get that into your head. I'm master and you damn well know it.'

'All right,' replied Mr. Spiller **meekly**, 'but **buzz off** to bed now, there's a good fellow. It's getting late and I'm tired.'

'You'll be tireder before **I've done with you**.' Mr. Gooch **thrust** both hands into his pockets and stood—a **bulky** and threatening figure—**swaying** rather dangerously. 'I'm short of cash,' he added. 'Had a bad week—**cleaned me out**. Time you **stumped up** a bit more.'

'Nonsense,' said Mr. Spiller, **with some spirit**. 'I pay you your **allowance** as we agreed, and let you come and stay here whenever you like, and that's all you get from me.'

'Oh, is it? Getting a bit **above yourself**, aren't you, Number **Bleeding** 4132?'

'**Hush**!' said Mr. Spiller, glancing hastily round as though the furniture had ears and tongues.

'Hush! hush!' repeated Mr. Gooch **mockingly**. 'You're in a good position to dictate terms, aren't you, 4132? Hush! The servants might hear! Betty might hear! Betty's young man might hear. Hah! Betty's young man—he'd be particularly pleased to know her father was an escaped **jail-bird**, wouldn't he? **Liable** at any moment **to** be **hauled back** to work out

---

rich F [rɪtʃ] großartig, köstlich **chuckle** ['tʃʌkl] (leises) Lachen **meek** [miːk] demütig, sanft **buzz off** sl. [bʌz] abschwirren **have done with s.o.** F [dʌn] mit j-m fertig sein **thrust** [θrʌst] stecken, schieben **bulky** ['bʌlkɪ] massig **sway** [sweɪ] schwanken, taumeln **clean out** sl. [kliːn] schröpfen, (aus)plündern **stump up** BE sl. [stʌmp] berappen, blechen **with some spirit** ['spɪrɪt] ziemlich energisch **allowance** [ə'laʊəns] (ausgesetzte) Summe, (bestimmter) Betrag **above o.s.** [ə'bʌv] hochmütig, stolz, selbstgefällig **bleeding** sl. ['bliːdɪŋ] verdammt, -flixt **hush!** [hʌʃ] still! pst! **mocking** ['mɒkɪŋ] spöttisch **jail-bird** F ['dʒeɪlbɜːd] Zuchthäusler **be liable to** ['laɪəbl] in Gefahr sein ... zu werden **haul back** [hɔːl] hier: zurückschleppen

his ten years' **hard** for **forgery**? And when I think,' added Mr. Gooch, 'that a man like me, that was only in for a short **stretch** and worked it out **good and proper**, is dependent on the **charity**—ha, ha!—of my dear friend 4132, while he's rolling in wealth—'

'I'm not rolling in wealth, Sam,' said Mr. Spiller, 'and you know **darn** well I'm not. But I don't want any trouble. I'll do what I can, if you'll **promise faithfully** this time that you won't ask for any more of these big sums, because my income won't stand it.'

'Oh, I'll promise that all right.' agreed Mr. Gooch cheerfully. 'You give me five thousand **down**—'

Mr. Spiller **uttered** a **strangled exclamation**.

'Five thousand? How do you suppose I'm to **lay hands on** five thousand all at once? Don't be an idiot, Sam. I'll give you a cheque for five hundred—'

'Five thousand,' insisted Mr. Gooch, '**or up goes the monkey**.'

'But I haven't got it, ' objected Mr. Spiller.

'Then you'd bloody well better find it,' returned Mr. Gooch.

'How do you expect me to find all that?'

'That's your **look-out**. You oughtn't to be so damned extravagant. Spending good money, that you ought to be giv-

---

hard = hard labour ['leɪbə] Zwangsarbeit **forgery** ['fɔːdʒərɪ] Fälschung **stretch** [stretʃ] Zeit(raum) **good and proper** F ['prɒpə] schön anständig **charity** ['tʃærɪtɪ] Mild-, Wohltätigkeit **darn** sl. [dɑːn] = **damn(ed)** verdammt, verflucht **promise faithfully** F ['prɒmɪs 'feɪθfʊlɪ] fest versprechen **down** [daʊn] (in) bar, sofort **utter** ['ʌtə] ausstoßen **strangled** ['stræŋgld] unterdrückt **exclamation** [ekskləˈmeɪʃn] (Auf)Schrei **lay hands on** [hændz] habhaft werden, hier: herbekommen **or up goes the monkey** BE sl. oder ich werde fuchtig **that's your look-out** das ist deine Sache

ing *me*, on fountains and stuff. Now, it's no good kicking Mr. Respectable 4132—I'm the man on top and **you're for it**, my **lad**, if you don't look after me properly. See?'

Mr. Spiller saw only too clearly. He saw, as he had seen indeed for some time, that his friend Gooch **had him by the short hairs**. He **expostulated** again feebly, and Gooch replied with a laugh and an offensive **reference to** Mrs. Digby.

*

Mr. Spiller did not realize that he had **struck** very hard. He hardly realized that he had struck at all. He thought he had **aimed a blow**, and that Gooch had **dodged** it and **tripped** over the leg of the **occasional table**. But he was not very clear in his mind, except on one point. Gooch was dead.

He had not fainted; he was not **stunned**. He was dead. He must have caught the **brass curb** of the **fender** as he fell. There was no blood, but Mr. Spiller, exploring the **inert** head with anxious fingers, found a spot above the **temple** where the bone **yielded** to pressure like a cracked egg-shell. The noise of the fall had been thunderous. Kneeling on the library floor, Mr. Spiller waited for the **inevtable** cry and footsteps from upstairs.

---

you're for it BE F hier: du bist dran **my lad** F [læd] hier: alter Knabe **have s.o. by the short hairs** sl. j-n beherrschen, j-n unter der Fuchtel haben **expostulate** [ɪks'pɒstjʊleɪt] protestieren **reference to** ['refrəns] Anspielung auf **struck** [strʌk] von **strike** [straɪk] zuschlagen **aim a blow (at)** [eɪm, bləʊ] e-n Schlag führen (gegen) **dodge** [dɒdʒ] ausweichen **trip** [trɪp] stolpern, straucheln **occasional table** [ə'keɪʒnəl] (Mehrzweck)Tischchen **stunned** [stʌnd] betäubt **brass curb** [brɑːs kɜːb] Messingvorsatz **fender** ['fendə] Kamingitter **inert** [ɪ'nɜːt] schlaff **temple** ['templ] Schläfe **yield** [jiːld] nachgeben **inevitable** [ɪn'evɪtəbl] unvermeidlich

Nothing happened. He remembered—with difficulty, for his mind seemed to be working slowly and **stiffly**—that above the library there was only the long **drawing-room**, and over that the **spare room** and bath-rooms. No **inhabited** bedroom looked out on that side of the house.

A slow, **grinding**, **grating** noise startled him. He **whisked round** hastily. The old-fashioned grandfather clock, **wheezing** as the hammer rose into action, struck eleven. He wiped the sweat from his forehead, got up and poured himself out another, and a stiffer, brandy.

The drink did him good. It seemed to take the brake off his mind, and the wheels **span** energetically. An extraordinary clarity took the place of his previous confusion.

He had murdered Gooch. He had not exactly **intended** to do so, but he had done it. It had not felt like murder, but there was not the slightest doubt what the police would think about it. And once he was in the hands of the police—Mr. Spiller shuddered. They would almost certainly want to take his fingerprints, and would be surprised to recognize a **bunch** of old friends.

Masters had heard him say that he would wait up for Gooch. Masters knew that everybody else had gone to bed. Masters would undoubtedly guess something. But stop!

---

stiff [stɪf] hier: zäh **drawing-room** ['drɔɪŋrʊm] Salon, Empfangszimmer **spare room** [speə rʊm] Gästezimmer **inhabited** [ɪn'hæbɪtɪd] bewohnt **grinding** ['graɪndɪŋ] schleifend **grating** ['greɪtɪŋ] knirschend **whisk round** [wɪsk raʊnd] hier: herumfahren **wheez** [wi:z] keuchen, schnaufen **span** [spæn] von **spin** [spɪn] hier: sich drehen **intend** [ɪn'tend] beabsichtigen, vorhaben **bunch** [bʌntʃ] Anzahl

Could Masters prove that he himself had gone to bed? Yes, probably he could. Somebody would have heard him cross the court and seen the light go up over the garage. One could not hope to **throw suspicion on** Masters—besides, the man hardly deserved that. But the mere idea had started Mr. Spiller's brain on a new and attractive line of thought.

What he really wanted was an alibi. If he could only confuse the police as to the time at which Gooch had died. If Gooch could be made to seem alive after he was dead ... somehow ...

He cast his thoughts back over stories he had read on holiday, dealing with this very matter. You **dressed up** as the dead man and **impersonated** him. You telephoned in his name. In the hearing of the butler, you spoke to the dead as though he were alive. You made a gramophone record of his voice and played it. You hid the body, and thereafter sent a forged letter from some distant place—

He paused for a moment. Forgery—but he did not want to start that old game over again. And all these things were too **elaborate**, or else impracticable at that time of night.

And then it came to him suddenly that he was a fool. Gooch must not be made to live later, but to die earlier. He should die before 10.30, at the time when Mr. Spiller, under the eyes of three observers, had been playing bridge.

---

throw suspicion on [θrəʊ, səs'pɪʃn] Verdacht lenken auf **dress up** [dres] verkleiden, hier: sich (so) anziehen **impersonate** [ɪm'pɜːsəneɪt] sich ausgeben für **elaborate** [ɪ'læbərɪt] kompliziert

So far, the idea was **sound** and **even**, in its **broad outline**, obvious. But now one had to come down to detail. How could he **establish** the time? Was there anything that had happened at 10.30?

He helped himself to another drink, and then, quite suddenly, as though lit by a floodlight, he saw his whole plan, **picked out vividly complete**, with every **join** and **angle** clear-cut.

He glanced at his watch; the **hands** stood at twenty minutes past eleven. He had the night before him.

He fetched an electric **torch** from the hall and stepped **boldly** out of the French window. Close beside it, against the wall of the house, were two taps, one ending in a **nozzle** for the **garden hose**, the other controlling the fountain at the bottom of the garden. This latter he turned on, and then without troubling to **muffle** his footsteps, followed the crazy-paved path down to the lilac hedge, and round by the bed of cotoneastes. The sky, despite the beauty of the early evening, had now turned very dark, and he could scarcely see the tall **column** of pale water above the dark shrubbery, but he heard its **comforting** splash and **ripple**, and as he stepped upon the surrounding grass, he felt the blown **spray** upon his face. The **beam** of the torch showed him the garden seat beneath the yews, and the tray, as he had expected, standing

---

sound [saʊnd] vernünftig, brauchbar **even** ['iːvən] einfach, unkompliziert **in broad outline** [brɔːd 'aʊtlaɪn] in groben Umrissen **establish** [ɪs'tæblɪʃ] festsetzen **pick out** [pɪk] herausgreifen, hervorheben **vividly complete** ['vɪvɪdlɪ kəm'pliːt] deutlich u. vollständig **join** [dʒɔɪn] Verbindungsstelle, Naht **angle** ['æŋgl] Winkel; Aspekt, Seite **hand** Zeiger (Uhr) **(electric) torch** BE [ɪ'lektrɪk tɔːtʃ] (Stab)Taschenlampe **bold** [bəʊld] mutig, beherzt **nozzle** ['nɒzl] Mundstück **garden hose** ['gɑːdn həʊz] Gartenschlauch **muffle** ['mʌfl] dämpfen **column of water** ['kɒləm, 'wɔːtə] Wassersäule **comforting** ['kʌmfətɪŋ] tröstlich **ripple** ['rɪpl] Rieseln, Plätschern **spray** [spreɪ] Gischt, Sprühregen **beam** [biːm] (Licht)Strahl

upon it. The whisky decanter was about half full. He emptied the greater part of its contents into the basin, **wrapping** the neck of the decanter in his handkerchief, so as to leave no fingerprints. Then, returning to the other side of the lilacs, he **satisfied himself** that the spray of the fountain was invisible from house or garden.

The next part of the **performance** he did not **care about**. It was risky; it might be heard; in fact, he wanted it to be heard if necessary—but it was a risk. He **licked** his dry lips and called the dead man by name:

'Gooch! Gooch!'

No answer, except the splash of the fountain, sounding to his anxious ear abnormally loud in the stillness. He glanced round, almost as though he expected the corpse to **stalk** awfully out upon him from the darkness, its head hanging and its dark mouth dropping open to show the pale gleam of its **dentures**. Then, pulling himself together, he walked **briskly** back up the path and, when he reached the house again, listened. There was no movement, no sound but the ticking of the clocks. He shut the library door gently. From now on there must be no noise.

There was a pair of **goloshes** in the **cloak-room** near the **pantry**. He put them on and slipped like a shadow through the French window again; then round the house into the

---

wrap [ræp] einwickeln **satisfy o.s.** ['sætɪsfaɪ] sich überzeugen od. vergewissern **performance** [pə'fɔːməns] Aus-, Durchführung **care about s.th.** [keə] sich et. machen aus **lick** [lɪk] lecken **stalk upon s.o.** [stɔːk] sich an j-n heranschleichen **denture** ['dentʃə] Gebiss; Pl Zähne **brisk** [brɪsk] rasch, flott; energisch **goloshes** Pl = **galoshes** Pl [gə'lɒʃɪz] Überschuhe **cloak-room** ['kləʊkrʊm] Garderobe **pantry** ['pæntrɪ] Speisekammer

courtyard. He glanced up at the garage; there was no light in the upper story and he **breathed a sigh of relief**, for Masters was **apt** sometimes to be **wakeful**. **Groping** his way to an **outhouse**, he switched the torch on. His wife had been an invalid for some years before her death, and he had brought her **wheeled chair** with him to 'The Pleasaunce', having a dim, sentimental **reluctance** to sell the thing. He was thankful for that, now; thankful, too, that he had **purchased** it from a good maker and that it ran so lightly and silently on its **pneumatic tyres**. He found the bicycle pump and blew the tyres up hard and, **for further precaution**, **administered** a drop of oil here and there. Then, with infinite precaution, he wheeled the chair round to the library window. How fortunate that he had put down stone **flags** and crazy paving everywhere, so that no wheel-tracks could show.

The job of getting the body through the window and into the chair **took it out of him**. Gooch had been a heavy man, and he himself was not in good training. But it was done at last. **Resisting** the impulse to run, he pushed his burden gently and **steadily** along the narrow **strip** of paving. He could not see very well, and he was afraid to flash his torch too often. A slip off the path into the herbaceous border would be fatal; he **set his teeth** and kept his gaze fixed steadily ahead of him. He felt as though, if he looked back at the house, he

---

breathe a sigh of relief [briːð, saɪ] erleichtert aufseufzen **be apt** [æpt] neigen **wakeful** ['weɪkfʊl] schlaflos **grope one's way** [grəʊp] sich vorwärts tasten **outhouse** ['aʊthaʊs] Nebengebäude **wheeled chair = wheel chair** [wiːl(d) tʃeə] Rollstuhl **reluctance** [rɪ'lʌktəns] Abneigung **purchase** ['pɜːtʃəs] kaufen **pneumatic tyres** Pl [njuː'mætɪk 'taɪəz] (Luft)Bereifung **for further precaution** ['fɜːðə prɪ'kɔːʃn] als weitere Vorsichtsmaßnahme **administer** [əd'mɪnɪstə] verabreichen, hier: verteilen **flag** [flæg] (Stein)Platte, Fliese **took it out of** von **take it out of** fertig machen, erschöpfen **resist** [rɪ'zɪst] widerstreben **steady** ['stedɪ] ruhig, gleichmäßig **strip** [strɪp] Streifen **set one's teeth** die Zähne zusammenbeißen

would see the upper windows **thronged** with staring white faces. The impulse to turn his head was almost **irresistible**, but he **determined** that he would not turn it.

At length he was round the edge of the lilacs and hidden from the house. The sweat was running down his face and the most **ticklish** part of his task was still to do. If he broke his heart in the effort, he must carry the body over the **plot of lawn**. No wheel-**marks** or heel marks or **signs of dragging** must be left for the police to see. He **braced** himself for the effort.

It was done. The corpse of Gooch lay there by the fountain, the **bruise** upon the temple carefully **adjusted** upon the sharp stone edge of the pool, one hand dragging in the water, the **limbs disposed** as naturally as possible, to look as though the man had stumbled and fallen. Over it, from head to foot, the water of the fountains sprayed, swaying and **bending** in the night wind. Mr. Spiller looked upon his work and saw that it was good. The journey back with the **lightened** chair was easy. When he had returned the vehicle to the outhouse and passed for the last time through the library window, he felt as though the burden of years had been rolled from his back.

His back! He had remembered to take off his **dinner-jacket** while **stooping** in the spray of the fountain, and only

---

thronged [θrɒŋd] gedrängt voll **irresistible** [ɪrɪ'zɪstəbl] unwiderstehlich **determine** [dɪ'tɜːmɪn] beschließen **ticklish** ['tɪklɪʃ] heikel, schwierig, kitz(e)lig **plot of lawn** [plɒt, lɔːn] Rasenstück **mark** [mɑːk] Spur, Abdruck **sign of dragging** [saɪn, 'drægɪŋ] hier: Schleifspur **brace o.s.** [breɪs] s-e Kräfte zusammennehmen **bruise** [bruːz] Quetschung, Beule, Prellung **adjust** [ə'dʒʌst] anpassen, hier: zurechtlegen **limbs** Pl [lɪmz] Gliedmaßen **dispose** [dɪs'pəʊz] anordnen, (zurecht)legen **bend** [bend] sich krümmen od. biegen **lightened** ['laɪtnd] leichter geworden **dinner-jacket** ['dɪnədʒækɪt] Smokingjacke **stoop** [stuːp] sich bücken

his shirt was **drenched**. That he could **dispose** of in the **linen-basket**, but the **seat** of his trousers gave him some uneasiness. He **mopped at** himself as best he could with his handkerchief. Then he made his calculations. If he left the fountain to play for an hour or so it would, he thought, produce the desired effect. Controlling his **devouring** impatience, he sat down and mixed himself a final brandy,

At 1 o'clock he rose, turned off the fountain, shut the library window with no more and no less than the usual noise and force, and went with **firm** footsteps up to bed.

*

Inspector Frampton was, to Mr. Spiller's delight, a highly intelligent officer. He picked up the **clues** thrown to him with the **eagerness** of a trained terrier. The dead man was last seen alive by Masters after dinner—8.30—just so. After which, the rest of the party had played bridge together till 10.30. Mr. Spiller had then gone out with Mrs. Digby. Just after he left, Masters had turned off the fountain. Mr. Proudfoot had left at 10.40 and Miss Spiller and the maids had then retired. Mr. Spiller had come in again at 10.45 or 10.50, and **inquired for** Mr. Gooch. After this, Masters had gone across to the garage, leaving Mr. Spiller to lock up. Later on, Mr. Spiller had gone

---

drenched [drentʃt] durchnässt **dispose of** wegschaffen, beseitigen **linen-basket** ['lɪnɪnbɑːskɪt] Wäschekorb **seat** [siːt] Hosenboden **mop at o.s.** [mɒp] an sich herumreiben od. -wischen **devouring** [dɪ'vaʊərɪŋ] verzehrend **firm** [fɜːm] fest **clue** [kluː] Anhaltspunkt, Spur **eagerness** ['iːgənɪs] Eifer **inquire for** [ɪn'kwaɪə] fragen nach

down the garden to look for Mr. Gooch. He had gone no farther than the lilac hedge, and there calling to him and getting no answer, had **concluded** that his guest had already come in and gone to bed. The housemaid **fancied** she had heard him calling Mr. Gooch. She placed this episode at about half past eleven—certainly not later. Mr. Spiller had **subsequently** sat up reading in the library till 1 o'clock, when he had shut the window and gone to bed also.

The body, when found by the gardener at 6.30 a.m., was still wet with the spray from the fountain, which had also **soaked** the grass beneath it. Since the fountain had been turned off at 10.30, this meant that Gooch must have lain there for an **appreciable** period before that. In view of the large quantity of whisky that he had drunk, it seemed probable that he had had a heart-attack, or had drunkenly stumbled, and, in falling, had struck his head on the edge of the pool. All these **considerations** fixed the time of death at from 9.30 to 10 o'clock—an opinion with which the doctor, though **declining to commit himself** within an hour or so, **concurred**, and the **coroner** entered a **verdict of accidental death**.

*

---

conclude [kən'klu:d] schließen, folgern **fancy** ['fænsɪ] glauben **subsequently** ['sʌbsɪkwəntlɪ] anschließend **soak** [səʊk] durchnässen **appreciable** [ə'pri:ʃəbl] geraum **consideration** [kənsɪdə'reɪʃn] Überlegung, Erwägung **decline** [dɪ'klaɪn] ablehnen **commit o.s.** [kə'mɪt] sich festlegen **concur with** [kən'kɜ:] übereinstimmen mit, beipflichten **coroner** ['kɒrənə] Untersuchungsrichter (in Fällen gewaltsamen od. plötzlichen Todes) **verdict of accidental death** ['vɜ:dɪkt, æksɪ'dentl deθ] hier: Urteil, das auf Tod durch Unfall lautete

Only the man who has been for years the helpless victim of **blackmail** could fully enter into Mr. Spiller's feelings. **Compunction** played no part in them—the relief was far too great. To be rid of the daily irritation of Gooch's presence, of his **insatiable** demands for money, of the **perpetual menace** of his drunken **malice**—these **boons** were well worth a murder. And, Mr. Spiller insisted to himself, as he sat **musing** on the rustic seat by the fountain, it had not really been murder. He determined to **call on** Mrs. Digby that afternoon. He could ask her to marry him now without **haunting** fear for the future. The scent of the lilac was **intoxicating**.

*

'Excuse me, sir,' said Masters.

Mr. Spiller, **withdrawing** his meditative gaze from the **spouting** water, looked inquiringly at the manservant, who stood in a respectful attitude beside him.

'If it is **convenient to** you, sir, I should wish to have my bedroom changed. I should wish to sleep indoors.'

'Oh?' said Mr. Spiller. 'Why that, Masters?'

'I **am subject to** be a light sleeper, sir, ever since the war, and I find the **creaking** of the weather-vane very **disturbing**.'

---

blackmail ['blækmeɪl] Erpressung **compunction** [kəm'pʌŋkʃn] Gewissensbisse Pl, Reue **insatiable** [ɪn'seɪʃəbl] unersättlich **perpetual** [pə'petʃʊəl] (be)ständig **menace** ['menəs] Bedrohung **malice** ['mælɪs] Bosheit **boon** [buːn] Segen; Pl Segnungen **musing** ['mjuːzɪŋ] in Gedanken versunken, sinnend **call on s.o.** [kɔːl] j-n besuchen **haunting** ['hɔːntɪŋ] quälend, beklemmend **intoxicating** [ɪn'tɒksɪkeɪtɪŋ] berauschend **withdraw from** sich entfernen; hier: lösen von **spouting** ['spaʊtɪŋ] heraus-, hervorschießend
be convenient to s.o. [kən'viːnjənt] j-m passen **be subject to** ['sʌbdʒɪkt] neigen zu **creaking** ['kriːkɪŋ] Quietschen, Knarren **disturbing** [dɪs'tɜːbɪŋ] störend

'It creaks, does it?'

'Yes, sir. On the night that Mr. Gooch **sustained** his unfortunate accident, sir, the wind changed at a quarter past eleven. The creaking woke me out of my first sleep, sir, and disturbed me very much.'

A coldness **gripped** Mr. Spiller at the **pit of the stomach**. The servant's eyes, in that moment, reminded him curiously of Gooch. He had never noticed any **resemblance** before.

'It's a curious thing, sir, if I may say so, that, with the wind **shifting** as it did at 11.15, Mr. Gooch's body should have become sprayed by the fountain. Up till 11.15, the spray was falling on the other side, sir. The **appearance presented** was as though the body had been placed in position subsequently to 11.15, sir, and the fountain turned on again.'

'Very strange,' said Mr. Spiller. On the other side of the lilac hedge, he heard the voices of Betty and Ronald Proudfoot, chattering as they paced **to and fro** between the herbaceous borders. They seemed to be happy together. The whole house seemed happier, now that Gooch was gone.

'Very strange indeed, sir. I may add that, after hearing the inspector's observations, I took the precaution to dry your **dress-trousers** in the linen-cupbord in the bath-room.'

'Oh, yes,' said Mr. Spiller.

---

sustain [səs'teɪn] erleiden **grip** [grɪp] ergreifen, packen **pit of the stomach** [pɪt, 'stʌmək] Magengrube **resemblance** [rɪ'zembləns] Ähnlichkeit **shift** [ʃɪft] wechseln, sich drehen **the appearance presented was ...** [ə'pɪərəns prɪ'zentɪd] hier: es (er)schien so ... **to and fro** [frəʊ] hin u. her, auf u. ab **dress-trousers** Pl ['drestraʊzəz] Hose des Abendanzugs

'I shall not, of course, mention the change of wind to the **authorities**, sir, and now that the **inquest** is over, it is not likely to occur to anybody, unless their attention should be drawn to it. I think, sir, all things being taken into consideration, you might find it worth your while to **retain** me **permanently** in your service at—shall we say double my present **wage** to begin with?'

Mr. Spiller opened his mouth to say, 'Go to Hell,' but his voice failed him. He bowed his head.

'I am much **obliged to** you, sir,' said Masters, and withdrew on silent feet.

Mr. Spiller looked at the fountain, with its tall water **wavering** and bending in the wind.

'Ingenious,' he muttered automatically, 'and it really costs nothing to run. It uses the same water over and over again.'

---

authorities Pl [ɔː'θɒrɪtɪz] Behörde(n Pl) **inquest** ['ɪnkwest] gerichtliche Verhandlung zur Feststellung der Todesursache (bei ungeklärten Todesfällen) **retain** [rɪ'teɪn] (be)halten **permanent** ['pɜːmənənt] ständig **wage** [weɪdʒ] (Arbeits)Lohn **be obliged to** [ə'blaɪdʒd] verbunden sein **waver** ['weɪvə] schwanken

A Lesson in Crime

By *G. D. H.* and *M. Cole*

Joseph Newton settled himself comfortably in his corner of a first-class **compartment** on the **Cornish** Riviera express. So far, he had the compartment to himself; and if, by strewing **rugs**, bags, books and papers about he could make himself look numerous enough to drive **fellow-travellers** away, there was hope he might remain **undisturbed**—for the long train was far from full. Let us take a look at him, and learn a little about him before his adventures begin—and end.

Age? Forty-five would not be **a bad guess**, though, in fact, he is rather less. As for his physical condition, '**well-nourished**' is a polite description; and we, who desire to have no illusions, can safely call him **paunchy**, and, without **positive grossness**, **flabby** with good living. His face is **puffy**, and whitish under the eyes; his mouth is loose, and **inclined** to **leer**.

His fair hair, which is rapidly growing thin, is **immaculately** brushed, and his clothes are **admirably** cut and **well-tended**, though he has not the art of wearing them well. Altogether he looks a **prosperous**, thoroughly self-satisfied,

---

compartment [kəm'pɑːtmənt] (Wagen)Abteil **Cornish** ['kɔːnɪʃ] Cornwall... **rug** [rʌg] Reisedecke **fellow-traveller** ['feləʊtrævlə] Mitreisende **undisturbed** ['ʌndɪs'tɜːbd] ungestört **a bad guess** schlecht geschätzt od. geraten **well-nourished** ['wel'nʌrɪʃt] wohlgenährt **paunchy** ['pɔːntʃɪ] dickbauchig **positive** ['pɒzətɪv] ausdrücklich, bestimmt **grossness** ['grəʊsnɪs] Grobheit **flabby** ['flæbɪ] schlaff **puffy** ['pʌfɪ] aufgedunsen **be inclined** [ɪn'klaɪnd] dazu neigen **leer** [lɪə] hier: schief grinsen **immaculate** [ɪ'mækjʊlɪt] makel-, tadellos **admirable** ['ædmərəbl] großartig **well-tended** ['wel'tendɪd] sehr gepflegt **prosperous** ['prɒspərəs] wohlhabend

and somewhat **self-indulgent** member of the British middle class; and that is precisely what he is.

His **walk in life**? You would put him down as a business man, possibly a merchant or a middle-sized employer, not a **professional man**. There you would be both right and wrong. He is a professional man, in a sense; and he is certainly in business.

In fact, he is Joseph Newton, the best-seller, whose crime stories and shockers were **plastered** all over the **bookstall** he had just left with his burden of newspapers under his arm. He has sold—heaven knows how many million copies of his stories, and his **serial rights**, first, second, and third, cost **fabulous** sums to **secure**.

But why describe him further? All the world knows him. And now he is on his way to Cornwall, where he has a pleasant little seaside cottage with twenty-seven bedrooms.

The train starts, and Newton's **carriage** still remains empty save for himself. He **heaves** a fat **sigh of relief** and picks up a magazine, in which he turns instinctively to a story by himself. For the moment he cannot remember who wrote it. **Poor stuff**, he thinks. He must find out which **'ghost'** was responsible, and **sack** him.

Joseph Newton was interrupted in his reflections at this point by the **consciousness** that someone was looking at

---

self-indulgent ['selfɪn'dʌldʒənt] nachgiebig gegen sich selbst **walk in life = walk of life** Beruf, soziale Schicht **professional man** [prə'feʃnəl mæn] Geistesarbeiter **plaster** ['plɑːstə] überschütten **bookstall** ['bʊkstɔːl] Zeitungsstand, -kiosk **serial rights** Pl ['sɪərɪəl raɪts] Copyright e-s Fortsetzungsromans **fabulous** ['fæbjʊləs] ungeheuer **secure** [sɪ'kjʊə] sich beschaffen **carriage** ['kærɪdʒ] Abteil **heave a sigh of relief** [hiːv, saɪ, rɪ'liːf] e-n Seufzer der Erleichterung ausstoßen **poor stuff** [pʊə stʌf] schlechtes Zeug **ghost = ghost-writer** ['gəʊstraɪtə] Ghostwriter (Schriftsteller, der für e-n anderen anonym schreibt) **sack** F [sæk] 'rausschmeißen **consciousness** ['kɒnʃəsnɪs] Bewusstsein

him. He glanced up and saw the figure of a man who was standing in the corridor and staring fixedly at him, with a curious **air of abstraction**. Newton stared back, trying to look as unwelcoming as possible. It would be really bad luck, he felt, if someone were to **invade** his compartment now.

The newcomer, after a moment more of staring, pushed back the door and came in, flinging down on top of one of Newton's bags a rug and a pillow done up in a **strap**. He seemed to have no other luggage. Newton unwillingly got up and **cleared** a corner of his **belongings**, and the stranger sat down and began to **unbuckle** his strap. Then he settled himself comfortably with the pillow behind his head, and closed his eyes. 'I hope to goodness he doesn't snore,' Newton thought.

While our second traveller is thus peacefully settling himself for a **doze**, we may as well take a good look at him also; for it may be important to know him later on. He is a **scraggy** little man, probably of sixty or more, with a completely bald pink head and a **straggling** grey beard which **emerges** from an incredibly folded and **puckered** yellow chin. His height is hardly more than five foot six, and his proportions are **puny**; but there is a **wiriness** about his **spare** person that contrasts strongly with Newton's fleshy **bulk**.

He is dressed, not so much ill as with a carelessness

---

air of abstraction [eə, æb'strækʃn] geistesabwesende Miene **invade** [ɪn'veɪd] eindringen in **strap** [stræp] Riemen **clear** [klɪə] frei machen **belongings** Pl [bɪ'lɒŋɪŋz] Habseligkeiten **unbuckle** ['ʌn'bʌkl] aufschnallen **doze** [dəʊz] leichter Schlummer **scraggy** ['skrægɪ] dürr, hager **straggling** ['stræglɪŋ] widerspenstig, unordentlich **emerge** [ɪ'mɜːdʒ] hervorsprießen **puckered** ['pʌkəd] runz(e)lig **puny** ['pjuːnɪ] klein, winzig **wiriness** ['waɪərɪnɪs] Drahtigkeit **spare** [speə] mager **bulk** [bʌlk] Körperfülle

amounting to eccentricity. His clothes, certainly cut by a good tailor, **hang in bags all over him**. His pockets **bulge**. His waistcoat is buttoned up wrong, and **sets awry**, and his shirt has come apart at the neck, so that a **disconsolate shirt-stud** is hanging out on one side, while his red tie is leaning towards the other. Moreover, the **sole** of one of his boots has come loose, and **flaps** helplessly as his crossed legs swing slowly to the rhythm of the train.

Yet, despite these appearances, the newcomer is certainly a gentleman, and one is inclined to **deem** him eccentric rather than poor. He might be an exceptionally **absent-minded** professor; though, as a matter of fact, he is not. But who he is Joseph Newton has no idea.

For some time there was silence in the compartment, as The Cornish Riviera **sped** westward past the long **spreading** ribbon of London. Newton's fellow-traveller did not snore. His eyes were closed whenever Newton glanced at him; and yet between whiles the **novelist** had still a **queer** feeling of being stared at. He told himself it was nonsense, and tried to bury himself in a Wild West story; but the **sensation** remained with him. Suddenly, as the train passed Maidenhead Station, his companion spoke, in a quiet positive voice, as of one used to telling idiots what idiots they were. A professorial voice, with a **touch** of **Scots** accent.

---

amount to [ə'maʊnt] hinauslaufen auf **hang in bags all over him** hier: sind überall ausgebeult **bulge** [bʌldʒ] sich ausbauchen **set** sitzen (Kleidung) **awry** [ə'raɪ] schief **disconsolate** [dɪs'kɒnsəlɪt] trostlos **shirt-stud** ['ʃɜːtstʌd] Hemdenknopf **sole** [səʊl] (Schuh)Sohle **flap** [flæp] hier: (herunter)baumeln **deem** [diːm] halten für **absent-minded** ['æbsənt'maɪndɪd] zerstreut **sped** [sped] von **speed** [spiːd] rasen, (dahin)eilen **spreading** ['spredɪŋ] sich ausdehnend **novelist** ['nɒvəlɪst] Romanschriftsteller **queer** [kwɪə] seltsam **sensation** [sen'seɪʃn] Gefühl **touch** [tʌtʃ] Anflug **Scots** [skɒts] schottisch

'Talking of murders,' it said, 'you have really no right to be so careless.'

'Eh?' said Newton, so **startled** that his magazine dropped from his hand to the floor. 'Eh, what's that?'

'I said you had no right to be so careless,' repeated the other.

Newton **retrieved** his magazine, and looked his fellow-traveller **contemptuously** up and down. 'I am not aware,' he said, 'that we were talking of murders, or of anything else for that matter.'

'There, you see,' said the other, 'You did hear what I said the first time. What I mean to say is that, if you expect intelligent people to read your stories, you might at least **trouble** to make them plausible.'

Newton **suppressed** the **rejoinder** that rose instantly to his lips. It was that he had far too large a circulation among fools to **bother about** what intelligent people thought. He only said, 'I doubt, sir, if you are **likely** to find my conversation any more satisfactory than my books,' and **resumed** his magazine.

'Probably not,' said the stranger. 'I expect success has **spoiled** you. But you had some brains to begin with. ... Those **Indian** stories of yours—'

Perhaps no other phrase would have **induced** Joseph

---

startled ['stɑːtld] überrascht **retrieve** [rɪ'triːv] hier: aufheben **contemptuous** [kən'temptjʊəs] geringschätzig, verächtlich **trouble** ['trʌbl] sich die Mühe machen **suppress** [sə'pres] unterdrücken **rejoinder** [rɪ'dʒɔɪndə] Erwiderung **bother about** ['bɒðə] sich kümmern um **likely** ['laɪklɪ] wahrscheinlich **resume** [rɪ'zjuːm] wieder aufnehmen **spoil** [spɔɪl] verderben **Indian** ['ɪndjən] indisch **induce** [ɪn'djuːs] veranlassen

Newton to **embark upon** a conversation with the stranger. But nobody nowadays ever read or bothered about his Indian stories, though he was very well aware that they were the best things he had ever done.

'—had **glimmerings** of quality,' the other was saying, 'and you might have **accomplished** something had you not taken to writing for money.'

'Are you aware, sir,' Newton said, 'that you are being excessively **rude**?'

'Quite,' 'I always am. It is so good for people. And really, in your last book, you have **exceeded** the limit.'

'Which of my last books are you talking about?' asked Newton, **hovering** between annoyance and amusement.

'It is called *The Big Noise*,' said the other, sighing softly.

'Oh, that,' said Newton.

'Now, in that book,' the stranger went on, 'you call the **heroine** Elinor and Gertrude on different pages. You cannot make up your mind whether her name was Robbins with two *b*'s or with one. You have killed the **corpse** in one place on Sunday and in another on Monday evening. That corpse was discovered twelve hours after the murder still **wallowing** in a **pool of wet blood**. The **coroner committed** no fewer than seventeen irregularities in conducting the **inquest**; and, finally, you have introduced three gangs, a mysterious China-

---

embark upon [ɪm'bɑːk] sich einlassen in **glimmering** ['glɪmərɪŋ] Schimmer **accomplish** [ə'kɒmplɪʃ] zustande bringen, erreichen **rude** [ruːd] unverschämt **exceed** [ɪk'siːd] überschreiten **hover** ['hɒvə] schwanken **heroine** ['herəʊɪn] Heldin **corpse** [kɔːps] Leiche **wallow** ['wɒləʊ] sich wälzen **pool of blood** [puːl, blʌd] Blutlache **coroner** ['kɒrənə] Untersuchungsrichter (in Fällen gewaltsamen od. plötzlichen Todes) **commit** [kə'mɪt] begehen **inquest** ['ɪnkwest] gerichtliche Verhandlung zur Feststellung der Todesursache

man, an unknown poison that leaves no **trace**, and a **secret society** of international Jews high up in the political world.'

The little old man held up his hands in horror as he ended the **grisly recital**.

'Well,' Newton asked, 'any more?'

'**Alas**, yes.' said the other. 'The **volume** includes, besides many **misprints**, fifteen **glaring inconsistencies**, nine cases of gross ignorance, and enough grammatical mistakes to stretch from Paddington to **Penzance**.'

This time Newton laughed outright. 'You seem to be a very earnest student of my writings,' he said.

The stranger picked up the rug from his knees and folded it **neatly** beside him. He removed the pillow, and laid that down too. He then moved across to the corner seat opposite Newton and, taking a **jewelled** cigarette-case from his pocket, selected a cigarette, returned the case to his pocket, found a match, lighted up, and began to smoke. Then he again drew out the case and offered it to Newton. 'Lavery's,' he said. 'I know your favourite brand.'

As a matter of fact, Newton never smoked Lavery's; but for a **handsome** sum he allowed his face, and a **glowing testimonial** to their **virtues**, to appear on their advertisements. Well, he might as well find out what the things were like. He took the **proffered** cigarette, and the stranger **obligingly**

---

trace [treɪs] Spur **secret society** ['siːkrɪt sə'saɪətɪ] Geheimbund **grisly** ['grɪzlɪ] schauerlich **recital** [rɪ'saɪtl] Aufzählung **alas** [ə'læs] leider!, ach! **volume** ['vɒljʊm] Band, Buch **misprint** ['mɪs'prɪnt] Druckfehler **glaring** ['gleərɪŋ] eklatant, krass **inconsistency** [ɪnkən'sɪstənsɪ] Widerspruch, Ungereimtheit **Penzance** [pen'zæns] Stadt in Cornwall **neat** [niːt] ordentlich, sauber **jewelled** ['dʒuːəld] mit Juwelen besetzt **handsome** ['hænsəm] ansehnlich, beträchtlich **glowing** ['gləʊɪŋ] begeistert **testimonial** [testɪ'məʊnjəl] Beurteilung, Gutachten **virtue** ['vɜːtjuː] Vorzug **proffered** ['prɒfəd] angeboten **obliging** [ə'blaɪdʒɪŋ] zuvorkommend

gave him a light. Newton puffed. Yes, they were good stuff—better than might be expected, though rather heavy.

'Now, in my view,' the stranger was saying, 'the essence of a really good murder is simplicity. All your books-all most people's books—have far too much **paraphernalia** about them. A really competent murderer would need no special **appliances**, and practically no preparations. **Ergo**, he would be in far less danger of leaving any **clues** behind him. Why, oh, why, Mr. Newton, do you not write murder story **on those lines**?'

Again Newton laughed. He was **disposed** to **humour** the old gentleman. 'It wouldn't make such a story,' he said, 'if the murderer really left no clues.'

'Oh, but there you are wrong,' said the other. 'What is needed is a perfectly simple murder, followed by a perfectly simple solution—so simple that only a great **mind** could think of it, by **penetrating** to the **utter** simplicity of the mind of the murderer.'

'I can't **abide** those psychological detectives,' Newton said. 'You'd better go and read Mr. **Van Dine**.' ('Or some of those fellows who would give their ears for a tenth of my **sales**,' his expression added.)

---

paraphernalia [pærəfə'neɪljə] Drum u. Dran **appliance** [ə'plaɪəns] (Hilfs)Mittel **ergo** ['ɜːgəʊ] lat. ergo, folglich **clue** [kluː] Anhaltspunkt, Spur **on those lines** [ðəʊz laɪnz] nach diesen Grundsätzen **disposed** [dɪs'pəʊzd] geneigt **humour s.o.** ['hjuːmə] j-m s-n Willen lassen; j-m mit Geduld ertragen **mind** [maɪnd] Verstand, Geist, Kopf **penetrate to** ['penɪtreɪt] vordringen bis zu **utter** ['ʌtə] äußerst, völlig **abide** [ə'baɪd] ausstehen **Van Dine** [væn daɪn] amerikanischer Kriminalschriftsteller der zwanziger Jahre **sale** [seɪl] Ab-, Umsatz

'Dear me, you quite misunderstand me. That wasn't what I meant at all. There would be no psychology in the story I have in mind. It would be more like **William Blake**'s poetry.'

'Mad, you mean,' said Newton.

'**Crystal sane**,' replied the other.

'Perhaps it will help you if I illustrate my point. Shall I **outline** the sort of murder I have in mind?'

'If you like,' said Newton, who found himself growing suddenly very sleepy.

'Very well,' said the stranger. 'Then I'll just draw down the **blinds**.'

He jumped up and lowered the blinds on the corridor side of the compartment.

'That's better,' he said. 'Now we shall be undisturbed. Now **supposing**—only supposing, of course—that there were two men in a railway carriage just like us, and they were perfect strangers, but one of them did not really care for the other's face—Are you listening, Mr. Newton?'

'Yes,' said Newton, very sleepily. He was now having real difficulty in keeping his eyes open.

'And, further, supposing neither of them had brought any special paraphernalia with him, except what any innocent traveller might be carrying—say, a rug, a pillow, and a rug-strap—'

William Blake ['wɪljəm bleɪk] englischer Dichter, Maler, Graphiker u. Mystiker (1757 bis 1827) **crystal sane** ['krɪstl seɪn] kristallklar u. völlig normal **outline** ['aʊtlaɪn] skizzieren, in groben Zügen darstellen **blind** [blaɪnd] Jalousie **supposing** [sə'pəʊzɪŋ] angenommen

As he spoke, the stranger picked up the rug-strap from the seat beside him.

'Hey, what's that about a rug-strap?' said Newton **roused** for a moment by a connection of ideas he was too sleepy **to sort out**.

'Except, of course, just one **doped** cigarette, containing an **opiate**—strong, but in no wise fatal,' the other went on **blandly**.

'What the—?' murmured Newton, struggling now **vainly** against an absolutely **stupefying drowsiness**.

'There would really be nothing to prevent him from committing a nice, neat murder, would there?' the old man continued, rising as he spoke with startling **agility** and flinging the **loop** of the rug-strap over Newton's head. 'Now would there?' he repeated, as he drew it tight around his victim's neck and neatly fastened it. Newton's mouth came wide open; his tongue **protruded**, and he began to **gurgle** horribly; his eyes **stuck out** from his head.

'And then,' said the stranger, 'the pillow would **come in so handy** to finish him off.' He dragged Newton down on the seat, placed the pillow firmly on his upturned face, and sat on it, smiling delightedly. The gurgling slowly **ceased**.

'The rug,' the cheerful voice went on, 'has proved to be **superfluous**. Really, Mr. Newton, murder is even easier than

---

rouse [raʊz] wachrütteln **sort out** [sɔːt] sortieren, einordnen **doped** [dəʊpt] hier: präpariert **opiate** ['əʊpɪɪt] Opiat, Schlafmittel **bland** [blænd] gelassen, kühl **vain** [veɪn] vergeblich **stupefying** ['stjuːpɪfaɪɪŋ] betäubend **drowsiness** ['draʊzɪnɪs] Schläfrigkeit **agility** [ə'dʒɪlɪtɪ] Beweglichkeit, Behendigkeit **loop** [luːp] Schlinge **protrude** [prə'truːd] heraustreten **gurgle** ['gɜːgl] gurgeln **stuck out** [stʌk] von **stick out** hervorstehen, hier: herausquellen **come in handy** gelegen kommen **cease** [siːs] aufhören **superfluous** [su(ː)'pɜːflʊəs] überflüssig

I supposed—though it is not often, I imagine, that a lucky chance **enables** one to do a service to the literary **craft** at the same time.'

Newton said nothing; for he was dead.

The stranger retained his position a little longer, still smiling gently to himself. Then he rose, removed the pillow from Newton's face, and, after a careful **survey** of the **body**, undid the strap. Next, he picked up a halfsmoked cigarette and threw it out of the window, folded his rug neatly, did it and the pillow up in the strap, and, opening the door into the corridor, walked quietly away **down the train.**

'What a pity!' he murmured to himself as he went. 'It would make such a good story, and I am afraid the poor fellow will never have the sense to write it.'

The body of Joseph Newton was **actually** discovered by a restaurant-car **attendant** who was going round to **collect** orders for the first lunch. Opening the door of a first-class compartment, which had all its blinds drawn down, he found Newton, no pleasant sight and **indubitably** dead, stretched out upon the seat where his companion had left him.

Without waiting to do more than make sure the man was dead, he **scuttled along** to fetch the **guard**. A brief **colloquy** of **train-officials** then took place in the fatal compartment, and it was decided to stop the train short of Newbury Sta-

---

enable s.o. [ɪ'neɪbl] es j-m ermöglichen **craft** [krɑːft] Zunft; Handwerk **survey** ['sɜːveɪ] Inspektion, Prüfung **body** ['bɒdɪ] Leiche **down the train** im Zug nach hinten **actually** ['æktʃʊəlɪ] in der Tat **attendant** [ə'tendənt] Bedienstete, Angestellte **collect** [kə'lekt] hier: entgegennehmen **indubitable** [ɪn'djuːbɪtəbl] unzweifelhaft, fraglos **scuttle along** ['skʌtl ə'lɒŋ] weiter-, forteilen **guard** [gɑːd] Zugführer; Schaffner **colloquy** ['kɒləkwɪ] Unterhaltung, Gespräch **train-official** ['treɪnə'fɪʃl] Zugbeamte

tion, and send for the police before anyone had a chance of leaving it. It seemed clear, as there had been no stop since they left Paddington, that the murderer must still be on it, unless he had leaped from an express travelling at full speed.

The police **duly** arrived, inspected the body, **hunted** the compartment in vain for traces of another passenger—for the murderer **had taken the precaution** of wearing gloves throughout his demonstration—took the name and address of every person on the train, to the number of some hundreds, had the carriage in which the murder had **occurred detached**, with much **shunting** and **grunting**, from the rest of the train, and finally allowed the delayed express to **proceed**.

Only those travellers who had been actually in the **coach** of which Newton's compartment had formed a part were kept back for further **inquiries**. But Newton's companion was not among them. Having given his correct name and address to the police, he proceeded quietly upon his journey in the empty first-class compartment two coaches farther back to which he had moved after his successful experiment in simplicity.

There were four hundred and ninety-eight passengers on the Cornish Riviera express whose names were taken by the police at Newbury; or, if you count Newton, four hundred and ninety-nine. Add guards and attendants, restaurant-car

---

duly ['du:lɪ] pünktlich **hunt for** [hʌnt] ab- od. durchsuchen nach **had taken the precaution** [prɪ'kɔ:ʃn] von **take the precaution** die Vorsichtsmaßnahme treffen **occur** [ə'kɜ:] sich ereignen, geschehen **detach** [dɪ'tætʃ] hier: abkoppeln **shunting** ['ʃʌntɪŋ] Rangieren **grunting** ['grʌntɪŋ] Murren **proceed** [prə'si:d] hier: s-e Reise fortsetzen **coach** [kəʊtʃ] Waggon, Wagen **inquiry** [ɪn'kwaɪərɪ] Ermittlung, Nachforschung, Frage

staff, and the **occupants** of a travelling **Post Office van**—total five hundred and nineteen.

Of these one hundred and twenty-six were women, one hundred and fifty-three children, and the rest men. That allowed for quite enough possible **suspects** for the police to follow up. They were followed up, **exhaustively**. But it did not apear that any single person among them had any **acquaintance** with Joseph Newton, or any connection with him save as readers of his books. Nor did a **meticulous** examination of Newton's past **suggest** the shadow of a reason why he should have been murdered.

The police tried their hardest, and the public and the Press did their best to assist, for the murder of a best-seller, by a criminal who left no clue, was enough to **excite** anybody's imagination. Several individuals, in their enthusiasm, went so far as to **confess** to the crime, and gave Scotland Yard several days' work in **disproving** their statement. But nothing helpful was **forthcoming**, and at long last the excitement died down.

It was more than three months later that the young Marquis of Queensferry **called upon** Henry Wilson, **formerly** the **chief** official of Scotland Yard, and now the **foremost** private detective in England. His **modest** request was that Wilson should solve for him the mystery of Joseph Newton's murder.

When Wilson asked him why he wanted it solved, the

---

occupant ['ɒkjʊpənt] Insasse **post office van** [pəʊst 'ɒfɪs væn] Postwagen **suspect** ['sʌspekt] Verdächtige **exhaustive** [ɪg'zɔːstɪv] erschöpfend, ganz gründlich **have any acquaintance with** [ə'kweɪntəns] irgendwie bekannt sein mit **meticulous** [mɪ'tɪkjʊləs] peinlich genau **suggest** [sə'dʒest] schließen lassen auf **excite** [ɪk'saɪt] erregen, hier: anregen **confess to** [kən'fes] gestehen **disprove** ['dɪs'pruːv] widerlegen **be forthcoming** [fɔːθ'kʌmɪŋ] zum Vorschein kommen **call upon s.o.** [kɔːl] e-n Besuch machen bei j-m **formerly** ['fɔːməlɪ] ehemals **chief** [tʃiːf] höchst(er, e, es) **foremost** ['fɔːməʊst] erst(er, e, es) **modest** ['mɒdɪst] bescheiden

Marquis explained that it was for a **bet**. It appeared that his old uncle, the **Honourable** Roderick Dominic **Acres-Noel**, had bet him fifty thousand pounds to a penny he could not solve the problem, and he, who had the title but not the money, would **be very willing to** lay his hands on fifty thousand pounds which his uncle, who had the money but not the title, would never miss. Asked the reason for so unusual a bet, he replied that the reason was Uncle Roderick, who was always betting on something, the sillier the better.

'Our family's like that, you know,' the Marquis added. 'We're all mad. And my uncle was quite excited about the case, because he was on the train when it happened. He even wrote to *The Times* about it.'

Wilson **rejected** the idea that he could solve a case which had utterly **baffled** Scotland Yard when the **trail** was fresh, now that it was stone cold, and all clues, **presumably**, **vanished into limbo**. Even the most **lavish** promises of **shares** in the fifty thousand pounds did not **tempt** him, and he **sent** the young Marquis **away with a flea in his ear**.

But, after the Marquis had gone, he found that he could not get the case out of his head. **In common with** everybody else, he had **puzzled his brains** over it at the time; but it was weeks since he had given it a thought. But now—here it was again—bothering his mind.

---

bet [bet] Wette **Honourable** ['ɒnərəbl] (der, die) Ehrenwerte **Acres-Noel** ['eɪkəz'nəʊəl] Familienname **be willing to do s.th.** ['wɪlɪŋ] gern et. tun **reject** [rɪ'dʒekt] zurückweisen **baffle** ['bæfl] verwirren, (j-m) ein Rätsel sein **trail** [treɪl] Spur, Fährte **presumable** [prɪ'zjuːməbl] vermutlich **vanish into limbo** ['vænɪʃ, 'lɪmbəʊ] hier: sich in Nichts auflösen **lavish** ['lævɪʃ] verschwenderisch **share** [ʃeə] Anteil **tempt** [tempt] in Versuchung führen **sent s.o. away with a flea in his ear** [fliː] von **send s.o. away ...** j-n abweisen, F j-n abfahren lassen **in common with** ['kɒmən] (genau) wie **puzzle one's brains** ['pʌzl] sich den Kopf zerbrechen

Hang it all, it wasn't reasonable—it was against nature—that a man should be able to murder another man and get away without leaving any clue at all. So, at any rate, the Marquis's crazy old uncle seemed to think, unless, indeed, he was **merely** crazy. Most likely he was.

Wilson could not say exactly at what moment he decided to **have one more shot at** this impossible mystery. Perhaps it was when he **recollected** that, according to the Marquis, Mr. Acres-Noel had himself travelled on that train to Cornwall. It might be that Mr. Acres-Noel had noticed something that the police had missed; he was just the sort of old gentleman who would enjoy keeping a **titbit of information** to himself. At any rate, it was one thing one could try.

Wilson rang up his old colleague, Inspector Blaikie, at Scotland Yard, and Blaikie **guffawed at** him.

'Solve it, **by all means**,' he said. 'We'll be delighted. We're sick of the sound of Newton's name. ... Yes, old Acres-Noel was on the train—I don't know anything more about him. ... Oh, **mad as a hatter**. Completely, ... Yes, he wrote to *The Times*, and they printed it. ... Three days afterwards, I think. Shall I have it looked up for you? ... Right you are. Let us know when you catch the murderer, won't you?'

Wilson sent for his own **file** of *The Times*, and looked up the letter of Mr. Acres-Noel. *The Times* had not thought it

---

mere [mɪə] bloß **have a shot at s.th.** [ʃɒt] es mit et. versuchen **recollect** [rekə'lekt] sich erinnern (an) **titbit of information** ['tɪtbɪt, ɪnfə'meɪʃn] informatorischer Leckerbissen **guffaw at s.o.** [gʌ'fɔː] j-n schallend auslachen **by all means** [miːnz] hier: wenn Sie durchaus wollen **mad as a hatter** ['hætə] total verrückt **file** [faɪl] hier: abgelegte (Zeitungs)Nummern Pl

worth the honour of the middle page, but fortunately had not **degraded** it into the **'Points' column**.

'Sir,' it ran,—

*'The methods of the police in **dealing with** the so-called Newton Mystery appear to show more than the usual official incompetence. As one of the passengers on the train on which Mr. Newton died, I have been **subjected** to **considerable annoyance**—and I may add compensated in part by some amusement—at the fruitless and irrelevant inquiries made by the police.*

*'It is **plain** the police have no **notion** of the motives which **prompted** the murder. Their inquiries show that. If they would **devote** more attention to thinking what the motive was, and less to the **accumulation** of useless information, the apparent complexity of the case would disappear. The truth is usually simple—too simple for idiots to see. Why was Newton murdered? Answer that, and it will appear plainly that only one person could have murdered him. Motive is essentially individual.*

'I am, yours, etc.,

'R.D. Acres-Noel.'

'Upon my word,' said Wilson to himself, 'that's a very **odd** letter.'

He read it several times over, staring at it as if the name of the murderer was written between the lines.

Suddenly he leaped to his feet, and with an excitement he

---

had not degraded it into [dɪ'greɪdɪd] hier: hatte ihn nicht zum Erscheinen in ... erniedrigt **points column** ['kɒləm] Spalte mit kleinerem Schriftgrad, in der die Fortsetzungen der im vorderen Teil abgedruckten Artikel gebracht werden **deal with** [diːl] sich beschäftigen od. befassen mit **subject to** [səb'dʒekt] aussetzen **considerable** [kən'sɪdərəbl] erheblich, beträchtlich **annoyance** [ə'nɔɪəns] Belästigung **plain** [pleɪn] klar **notion** ['nəʊʃn] Vorstellung **prompt** [prɒmpt] eingeben; hier: führen zu **devote** [dɪ'vəʊt] schenken **accumulation** [əkjuːmjʊ'leɪʃn] Anhäufung **odd** [ɒd] merkwürdig, komisch

seldom showed, **dashed** down **Whitehall** to Inspector Blaikie's office. Within ten minutes he was **making a proposition** to that official which left him **starkly incredulous**.

'I know,' Wilson **persisted**, 'it isn't a certainty, it's a thousand to one chance. But it *is* a chance, and I want to try it. I'm not asking the **Department** to **commit itself** in any way, only to let me have a couple of men standing by. Don't you see, the whole point about this extraordinary letter is the way it **stresses** the question of motive? And, more than that, it suggests that the writer knows what the motive was. Now, how could he do that unless—'

'But, if that's so, the man's mad!' Blaikie protested. 'Whoever heard of anyone murdering a complete stranger just to *show* him?'

'Well, he certainly is mad, isn't he? You said so yourself, and his family's **notoriously** crazy.'

'He'll have to be pretty well **off his rocker**,' Blaikie remarked, 'if he's to be kind enough to come and **shove** his neck in a **noose** for you.'

'One can but try,' Wilson said. 'If you won't help me I'm going to try alone. I must have one shot at getting to the bottom of it.' And eventually Blaikie agreed.

The **upshot** was that Wilson, immediately after his interview, arranged for the posting of the following letter, **forged**

---

dash [dæʃ] stürmen **Whitehall** ['waɪt'hɔːl] Straße in London, Sitz der Ministerien **make a proposition** [prɒpə'zɪʃn] e-e Behauptung aufstellen **stark** [stɑːk] völlig **incredulous** [ɪn'kredjʊləs] ungläubig **persist** [pə'sɪst] beharren **department** [dɪ'pɑːtmənt] hier: Polizeibehörde **commit o.s.** [kə'mɪt] sich binden od. festlegen **stress** [stres] betonen **notorious** [nəʊ'tɔːrɪəs] notorisch, wie jeder weiß **off one's rocker** sl. ['rɒkə] verrückt **shove** [ʃʌv] stecken **noose** [nuːs] Schlinge **upshot** ['ʌpʃɒt] Ergebnis, Ende **forge** [fɔːdʒ] fälschen

with extreme care so as to imitate the handwriting of the **supposed** author. It was **dispatched** from the **pillar-box** nearest to Joseph Newton's Cornish cottage.

'Dear Mr. Acres-Noel,' it said, —

'Ever since our ***chance meeting*** *a few months ago, I have been thinking over the very interesting demonstration you were kind enough to give me on that occasion. May I confess, however, that I am still not quite satisfied; and I should be even more deeply* ***obliged*** *if I could induce you repeat it. As it happens, I shall be returning to London this week-end, and travelling down again to Cornwall on the Riviera express next Wednesday. If you too should chance to be travelling that way, perhaps we may meet again.*

'Yours very truly,

'Joseph Newton.'

Someone **remarkably** like the **late** Joseph Newton settled himself comfortably in the corner of a first-class compartment in the Cornish Riviera express. He had the compartment to himself, and although the train had begun to fill up, no other traveller had entered when the train drew out of the station. Very discreetly, passengers who came near it had been **warned away** by the station officials.

---

supposed [sə'pəʊzd] vermeintlich, angeblich **dispatch** [dɪs'pætʃ] abschicken **pillar-box** BE ['pɪləbɒks] Briefkasten (in Säulenform) **chance meeting** ['mi:tɪŋ] zufälliges Zusammentreffen **be obliged** [ə'blaɪdʒd] zu Dank verpflichtet sein **remarkable** [rɪ'mɑ:kəbl] bemerkenswert, auffallend **late** [leɪt] verstorben **warn away** = warn off [wɔ:n] fernhalten

The train had not yet gathered its full speed when the **solitary** traveller became conscious that someone was standing outside the compartment, and staring in at him. He raised his eyes from the magazine he was reading, and looked back. Slowly, the newcomer pushed back the **sliding door**, entered the compartment, and sat down in the far corner.

He was a little old man, with a straggling beard, wearing very shabby clothes. He flung down on the seat beside him a rug and a pillow tied up in a strap. Undoing his bundle, he settled himself with the pillow behind his head, the rug over his knees, and the strap on the seat beside him. Then he closed his eyes.

Wilson did and said nothing. It was nervous work, waiting for his **cue**. But by this time he knew he was right. The millionth chance had come off.

The train **flashed** at length—it seemed hours—through Maidenhead Station. Suddenly the old man spoke.

'Talking of murders,' he said, 'it is my turn to apologize. I am afraid I **bungled** it last time.'

'Not at all,' said Wilson, hoping that his voice would not **give him away**; 'but if you would kindly just show me again how—'

'With pleasure,' said the old man.

---

solitary ['sɒlɪtərɪ] einsam **sliding door** ['slaɪdɪŋ] Schiebetür **cue** [kju:] Stichwort **flash** [flæʃ] rasen **bungle** ['bʌŋgl] verpfuschen, -patzen **give away** verraten

He moved **with alacrity** to the corner opposite Wilson, took from his pocket a jewelled cigarette-case, and proffered it. Wilson took a cigarette, and did a second's rapid thinking before the match was produced. A cigarette was something he had not allowed for, and it might even turn out to be poisoned. However, no use to hesitate now. He **suffered** Mr. Acres-Noel to light it, and the heavy sweetish taste **confirmed** his fears.

Fortunately, however, it was hardly alight before the other rose and went to the window.

'You won't mind my pulling down the blinds, will you?' he said; and Wilson took advantage of his movement to **effect** a **lightning** exchange of the suspicious cigarette for one of his own. This was a relief, but clearly he must show some signs of being affected by it. Sleepiness seemed the most likely **clue**. He yawned.

'You follow me so far, I **trust**,' said the other.

'Perfectly,' said Wilson slowly. 'Please—go—' Slowly his eyes closed, and his head began to **wag**.

The old man seized the rug-strap.

'This is the next step,' he said, **attempting** to **cast** it over Wilson's head. But Wilson sprang to his feet, **warded off** the strap, and pressed a button beside him which had been fixed to communicate with the **adjoining** compartment.

---

with alacrity [ə'lækrɪtɪ] bereitwillig **suffer** ['sʌffə] gestatten **confirm** [kən'fɜːm] bestätigen **effect** [ɪ'fekt] vornehmen **lightning** ['laɪtnɪŋ] blitzschnell **clue** [kluː] Schlüssel (zum Erfolg) **trust** [trʌst] hoffen **wag** [wæg] wackeln **attempt** [ə'tempt] versuchen **cast** [kɑːst] werfen **ward off** [wɔːd]] abwehren **adjoining** [ə'dʒɔɪnɪŋ] angrenzend, Nachbar..., Neben...

Almost as he **grappled** with his now **frenzied** antagonist, two **stalwart** policemen **in plain clothes** rushed in **to his aid**. Mr. Acres-Noel, **alternately** protesting his innocence and shrieking with wild laughter, was soon safely secured. The train slowed down and stopped at the **deserted** station of Newbury **Racecourse**, where **captors** and **captive** descended almost unnoticed. Then it sped upon its way.

Mr. Acres-Noel, safe in **Broadmoor**, has only one complaint. The authorities will not **supply** him with Joseph Newton's new books. He wants to see whether that popular writer has **benefited** by his lesson in practical criminology.

---

grapple ['græpl] ringen **frenzied** ['frenzɪd] rasend, tobend **stalwart** ['stɔːlwət] kräftig **in plain clothes** [kləʊðz] in Zivil **(rushed) to his aid** [eɪd] ... und eilten ihm zu Hilfe **alternately** [ɔːl'tɜːnɪtlɪ] abwechselnd **deserted** [dɪ'zɜːtɪd] verlassen **racecourse** ['reɪskɔːs] Rennbahn **captors** Pl ['kæptəz] hier: die, die ihn gefangen nahmen **captive** ['kæptɪv] hier: der Gefangene **Broadmoor** ['brɔːdmʊə] Anstalt für kriminelle Geisteskranke in Berkshire, England ['bɑːkʃɪə] **supply** [sə'plaɪ] versorgen **benefit by** ['benɪfɪt] Nutzen ziehen aus

The Telltale Heart

By *Edgar Allan Poe*

True!—nervous—very, very **dreadfully** nervous I had been and am; but why *will* you say that I am mad? The **disease** had **sharpened** my senses—not destroyed—not **dulled** them. Above all was the sense of hearing **acute**. I heard all things in the heaven and in the earth. I heard many things in hell. How, then, am I mad? **Hearken**! And observe how **healthily**—how calmly I can tell you the whole story.

It is impossible to say how first the idea entered my brain; but once **conceived**, it **haunted** me day and night. **Object** there was none. Passion there was none. I loved the old man. He had never **wronged** me. He had never **given me insult**. For his gold I had no desire. I think it was his eye! Yes, it was this! One of his eyes resembled that of a **vulture**—a **pale blue** eye, with a **film** over it. Whenever it fell upon me, **my blood ran cold**; and so **by degrees**—very gradually—I made up my mind to take the life of the old man, and **thus rid myself of** the eye for ever.

Now this is the point. You **fancy** me mad. Madmen know nothing. But you should have seen *me*. You should have seen how wisely I **proceeded**—with what **caution**—with what

---

telltale ['telteɪl] verräterisch **dreadful** ['dredfʊl] furchtbar **disease** [dɪ'ziːz] Krankheit **sharpen** ['ʃɑːpən] schärfen **dull** [dʌl] abstumpfen **acute** [ə'kjuːt] hier: fein **hearken!** ['hɑːkən] (poetisch:) hör(en Sie) zu od. her! **healthy** ['helθɪ] hier: geistig gesund, vernünftig **conceive** [kən'siːv] von **conceive an idea** auf e-n Gedanken kommen, hier: daraufkommen **haunt** [hɔːnt] verfolgen, quälen **object** ['ɒbdʒɪkt] hier: Gegner **wrong s.o.** [rɒŋ] j-n ungerecht behandeln, j-m Unrecht tun **had given me insult** ['ɪnsʌlt] von **give s.o. insult** j-n beleidigen **vulture** ['vʌltʃə] Geier **pale blue** [peɪl] blassblau **film** [fɪlm] dünnes Häutchen, Film **my blood ran cold** das Blut erstarrte mir in den Adern **by degrees** [dɪ'griːz] nach u. nach **thus** [ðʌs] so **rid o.s. of** [rɪd] sich befreien od. frei machen von **fancy** ['fænsɪ] glauben **proceed** [prə'siːd] vorgehen **caution** ['kɔːʃn] Vorsicht

foresight—with what **dissimulation** I went to work! I was never kinder to the old man than during the whole week before I killed him. And every night, about midnight, I turned the **latch** of his door and opened it—oh, so gently! And then, when I had made an opening **sufficient** for my head, I put in a dark **lantern**, all closed, closed, so that no light shone out, and then I thrust in my head. Oh, you would have laughed to see how **cunningly** I thrust it in! I moved it slowly—very, very slowly, so that I might not disturb the old man's sleep. It took me an hour to place my whole head within the opening so far that I could see him as he lay upon his bed. Ha!—would a madman have been so wise as this? And then, when my head was well in the room, I undid the lantern cautiously—oh, so cautiously—cautiously (for the **hinges creaked**)—I undid it just so much that a single thin **ray** fell upon the vulture eye. And this I did for seven long nights—every night just at midnight—but I found the eye always closed; and so it was impossible to do the work; for it was not the old man who **vexed** me, but his **Evil Eye**. And every morning, when the day broke, I went **boldly** into the chamber, and spoke **courageously** to him, calling him by name in a hearty tone, and **inquiring** how he had passed the night. So you see he would have been a very **profound** old man, indeed, to suspect that every night, just at twelve, I looked in upon him while he slept.

---

foresight ['fɔːsaɪt] Vorsorge **dissimulation** [dɪsɪmjʊ'leɪʃn] Verstellung, Heuchelei **latch** [lætʃ] hier: Türgriff **sufficient** [sə'fɪʃnt] ausreichend, genügend **lantern** ['læntən] Laterne **cunning** ['kʌnɪŋ] schlau, geschickt, listig **hinge** [hɪndʒ] (Tür)Angel **creak** [kriːk] quietschen **ray** [reɪ] (Licht)Strahl **vex** [veks] ärgern, irritieren **evil eye** ['iːvl] böser Blick, hier: böses Auge **bold** [bəʊld] kühn, keck, dreist **courageous** [kə'reɪdʒəs] beherzt, mutig **inquire** [ɪn'kwaɪə] sich erkundigen **profound** [prə'faʊnd] scharfsinnig

Upon the eighth night I was more than usually cautions in opening the door. A watch's minute hand moves more quickly than did mine. Never before that night had I *felt* the **extent** of my own powers—of my **sagacity**. I could scarcely **contain** my feelings of triumph. To think that there I was, opening the door, little by little, and he not even to dream of my secret deeds or thoughts. I **fairly chuckled** at the idea; and perhaps he heard me; for he moved on the bed suddenly, as if **startled**. Now you may think that I drew back—but no. His room was as **black as pitch** with the thick darkness (for the **shutters** were close fastened, **through fear of** robbers), and so I knew that he could not see the opening of the door, and I kept pushing it on **steadily**, steadily.

I had my head in, and was about to open the lantern, when my thumb **slipped** upon the **tin** fastening, and the old man sprang up in the bed, crying out—"Who's there?"

I kept quite still and said nothing. For a whole hour I did not move a muscle, and in the meantime I did not hear him lie down. He was still sitting up in the bed listening;—just as I have done, night after night, hearkening to the **death watches** in the wall.

Presently I heard a slight groan, and I knew it was the groan of **mortal terror**. It was not a groan of pain or of **grief**—oh, no!—it was the low **stifled** sound that arises

---

extent [ɪks'tent] Ausmaß **sagacity** [sə'gæsɪtɪ] Klugheit, Scharfsinn **contain** [kən'teɪn] zügeln **fairly** ['feəlɪ] geradezu, direkt **chuckle** ['tʃʌkl] (stillvergnügt) in sich hineinlachen **startled** ['stɑːtld] aufgeschreckt **as black as pitch** [pɪtʃ] pechschwarz **shutter** ['ʃʌtə] Fensterladen **through fear of** [θruː fɪə] aus Furcht vor **steady** ['stedɪ] stetig, ständig; ruhig **slip** [slɪp] ausgleiten **tin** [tɪn] Zinn..., Blech... **death watch** [deθ] Totenuhr **mortal terror** ['mɔːtl 'terə] Todesangst **grief** [griːf] Kummer, Leid **stifled** ['staɪfld] erstickt, unterdrückt

from the bottom of the soul when **overcharged with awe**. I knew the sound well. Many a night, just at midnight, when all the world slept, it has **welled up** from my own **bosom**, deepening, with its dreadful echo, the terrors that **distracted** me. I say I knew it well. I knew what the old man felt, and pitied him, although I chuckled at heart. I knew that he had been lying awake ever since the first slight noise, when he had turned in the bed. His fears had been ever since growing upon him. He had been trying to fancy them **causeless**, but could not. He had been saying to himself—"It is nothing but the wind in the chimney—it is only a mouse crossing the floor," or "it is merely a **cricket** which has made a single **chirp**." Yes, he has been trying to **comfort** himself with these **suppositions**; but he had found all **in vain**. *All in vain;* because Death, in approaching him, had **stalked** with his black shadow before him, and **enveloped** the victim. And it was the **mournful** influence of the **unperceived** shadow that caused him to feel—although he neither saw nor heard—to *feel* the presence of my head within the room.

When I had waited a long time, very patiently, without hearing him lie down, I **resolved** to open a little—a very, very little **crevice** in the lantern. So I opened it—you cannot imagine how **stealthily**, stealthily—until, at length, a single

---

overcharged with awe ['əʊvə'tʃɑːdʒd, ɔː] hier: voller Furcht, furchtbeladen **well up** aufsteigen **bosom** ['bʊzəm] Busen, Brust, Herz **distract** [dɪs'trækt] quälen, peinigen **causeless** ['kɔːzlɪs] grundlos, unbegründet **cricket** ['krɪkɪt] Heimchen, Grille **chirp** [tʃɜːp] Gezirp **comfort** ['kʌmfət] trösten, beruhigen **supposition** [sʌpə'zɪʃn] Vermutung **in vain** [veɪn] vergebens, umsonst **stalk** [stɔːk] einherstolzieren **envelop** [ɪn'veləp] einhüllen, hier: (bereits) umklammern **mournful** ['mɔːnfʊl] düster **unperceived** ['ʌnpə'siːvd] unbemerkt **resolve** [rɪ'zɒlv] beschließen **crevice** ['krevɪs] Spalt **stealthy** ['stelθɪ] verstohlen

dim ray, like the thread of the spider, shot from out the crevice and full upon the vulture eye.

It was open—wide, wide open—and I grew furious as I **gazed upon** it. I saw it **with perfect distinctness**—all a **dull** blue, with a **hideous veil** over it that **chilled the very marrow in my bones**; but I could see nothing else of the old man's face or person: for I had directed the ray as if by instinct, precisely upon the damned spot.

And now have I not told you that what you mistake for madness is but over-acuteness of the senses?—now, I say, there came to my ears a low, dull, quick sound, such as a watch makes when enveloped in cotton. I knew *that* sound well too. It was the beating of the old man's heart. It **increased** my fury, as the beating of a drum stimulates the soldier into courage.

But even yet I **refrained** and kept still. I scarcely breathed. I held the lantern motionless. I tried how steadily I could **maintain** the ray upon the eye. Meantime the **hellish tattoo** of the heart increased. It grew quicker and quicker, and louder and louder every **instant**. The old man's terror *must* haven been extreme! It grew louder, I say, louder every moment!—do you **mark** me well? I have told you that I am nervous: so I am. And now at the **dead** hour of the night, **amid** the dreadful silence of that old house, so strange a

---

dim [dɪm] schwach, trüb **gaze upon** [geɪz] starren auf **with perfect distinctness** ['pɜːfɪkt dɪs'tɪŋktnɪs] in aller Deutlichkeit, ganz klar **dull** [dʌl] matt, trüb **hideous** ['hɪdɪəs] gräßlich, abscheulich **veil** [veɪl] Schleier **chill** [tʃɪl] frösteln od. erschauern lassen **the very marrow in my bones** ['mærəʊ, bəʊnz] selbst das Mark in m-n Knochen, hier: mein Innerstes **increase** [ɪn'kriːs] (sich) steigern od. vergrößern **refrain** [rɪ'freɪn] sich beherrschen od. zurückhalten **maintain** [meɪn'teɪn] hier: richten **hellish** ['helɪʃ] höllisch, teuflisch **tattoo** [tə'tuː] Klopfen, Trommeln **instant** ['ɪnstənt] Augenblick **mark** [mɑːk] sich merken, hier: zuhören **dead** [ded] hier: ruhig **amid** [ə'mɪd] (mitten) in

noise as this **excited** me to uncontrollable terror. Yet, for some minutes longer I refrained and stood still. But the beating grew louder, louder! I thought the heart must burst. And now a new **anxiety** seized me—the sound would be heard by a neighbor! The old man's hour had come! With a loud yell, I threw open the lantern and leaped into the room. He **shrieked** once—once only. In an instant I **dragged** him to the floor, and pulled the heavy bed over him. I then smiled gaily, to find the deed so far done. But, for many minutes, the heart beat on with a **muffled** sound. This, however, did not vex me; it would not be heard through the wall. At length it **ceased**. The old man was dead. I removed the bed and examined the corpse. Yes, he was stone, stone dead. I placed my hand upon the heart and held it there many minutes. There was no **pulsation**. He was stone dead. His eye would **trouble** me no more.

If still you think me mad, you will think so no longer when I describe the wise precautions I took for the **concealment** of the body. The night **waned**, and I worked hastily, but in silence. First of all I **dismembered** the corpse. I cut off the head and the arms and the legs.

I then took up three **planks** from the **flooring** of the chamber, and **deposited** all between the **scantlings**. I then replaced the boards so cleverly, so cunningly, that no human

---

excite to [ɪk'saɪt] versetzen in **anxiety** [æŋ'zaɪətɪ] Angst **shriek** [ʃriːk] aufschreien **drag** [dræg] zerren **muffled** ['mʌfld] gedämpft **cease** [siːs] aufhören **pulsation** [pʌl'seɪʃn] Schlagen, Pochen **trouble** ['trʌbl] belästigen; quälen **concealment** [kən'siːlmənt] Verbergen, Verstecken **wane** [weɪn] zu Ende gehen **dismember** [dɪs'membə] zerstückeln **plank** [plæŋk] Diele **flooring** ['flɔːrɪŋ] Fußboden **deposit** [dɪ'pɒzɪt] unterbringen **scantling** ['skæntlɪŋ] Latte

eye—not even his—could have **detected** any thing wrong. There was nothing to wash out—no **stain** of any kind—no blood-spot whatever. I had been too **wary** for that. A **tub** had caught all—ha! ha! When I had made an end of these labors, it was four o'clock—still dark as midnight. As the bell **sounded the hour**, there came a knocking at the street door. I went down to open it with a light heart,—for what had I *now* to fear? There entered three men, who introduced themselves, with perfect **suavity**, as officers of the police. A shriek had been heard by a neighbor during the night; **suspicion** of **foul play** had been aroused; **information** had been **lodged** at the police office, and they (the officers) had been **deputed** to search the **premises**.

I smiled,—for *what* had I to fear? I **bade** the gentlemen **welcome**. The shriek, I said, was my own in a dream. The old man, I mentioned, was absent in the country. I took my visitors all over the house. I bade them search—search *well*. I led them, at length, to *his* chamber. I showed them his **treasures**, **secure**, **undisturbed**. In the enthusiasm of my **confidence**, I brought chairs into the room, and desired them *here* to rest from their **fatigues**, while I myself, in the wild **audacity** of my perfect triumph, placed my own seat upon the very spot beneath which **reposed** the corpse of the victim.

The officers were satisfied. My ***manner*** had convinced

---

detect [dɪ'tekt] entdecken, finden **stain** [steɪn] Fleck **wary** ['weərɪ] vor-, umsichtig **tub** [tʌb] Zuber, Wanne **sound the hour** [saʊnd] die volle Stunde schlagen **suavity** ['swɑːvɪtɪ] Höflichkeit **suspicion** [səs'pɪʃn] Verdacht **foul play** [faʊl pleɪ] Verbrechen **information had been lodged** [ɪnfə'meɪʃn, lɒdʒd] von **lodge information** Anzeige erstatten **depute** [dɪ'pjuːt] beauftragen **premises** Pl ['premɪsɪz] hier: Haus, Räumlichkeiten Pl **bade … welcome** [bæd 'welkəm] von **bid s.o. welcome** j-n willkommen heißen **treasures** Pl ['treʒəz] Reichtümer, Schätze **secure** [sɪ'kjʊə] sicher, in Sicherheit **undisturbed** ['ʌndɪs'tɜːbd] unangetastet, unberührt **confidence** ['kɒnfɪdəns] Selbstvertrauen; Dreistigkeit **fatigues** Pl [fə'tiːgz] mühselige Arbeit, Strapaze **audacity** [ɔː'dæsɪtɪ] Kühnheit, Verwegenheit **repose** [rɪ'pəʊz] ruhen **manner** ['mænə] Auftreten, Verhalten

them. I was **singularly at ease**. They sat, and while I answered **cheerily**, they chatted familiar things. But, **ere long**, I felt myself getting pale and wished them gone. My head ached, and I fancied a ringing in my ears: but still they sat and still chatted. The ringing became more distinct:—it continued and became more distinct: I talked more freely to get rid of the feeling: but it continued and gained definitiveness—until, at length, I found that the noise was *not* within my ears.

No doubt I now grew *very* pale;—but I talked more fluently, and with a **heightened** voice. Yet the sound increased—and what could I do? It was *a low, dull, quick sound—much such a sound as a watch makes when enveloped in cotton*. I **gasped for breath**—and yet the officers heard it not. I talked more quickly—more vehemently; but the noise steadily increased. I arose and **argued** about **trifles**, in **a high key** and with violent gesticulations, but the noise steadily increased. Why *would* they not be gone! I **paced** the floor **to and fro** with heavy **strides**, as if excited to fury by the observation of the men—but the noise steadily increased. Oh God! what *could* I do? I **foamed**—I **raved**—I swore! I swung the chair upon which I had been sitting, and **grated** it **upon** the boards, but the noise arose over all and continually increased. It grew louder—louder—*louder!* And still the men

---

singularly ['sɪŋgjʊləlɪ] ungewöhnlich **at ease** [iːz] entspannt, gelöst **cheery** ['tʃɪərɪ] vergnügt, munter **ere long** [eə lɒŋ] (poetisch:) bald **heightened** ['haɪtnd] hier: erhoben **gasp for breath** [gɑːsp, breθ] nach Luft ringen **argue** ['ɑːgjuː] debattieren, streiten **trifle** ['traɪfl] Kleinigkeit **in a high key** [haɪ kiː] in hohem Ton(fall), hier: schrill **pace the floor to and fro** [peɪs, flɔː, frəʊ] im Zimmer auf u. ab gehen **stride** [straɪd] (großer) Schritt **foam** [fəʊm] schäumen (vor Wut) **rave** [reɪv] rasen, toben **grate it upon** [greɪt] hier: damit knirschend fahren über

chatted **pleasantly**, and smiled. Was it possible they heard not? Almighty God!—no, no! They hear!—they suspected!—they *knew!*—they were **making a mockery of** my horror!— this I thought, and this I think. But any thing was better than this **agony**! Any thing was more tolerable than this **derision**! I could bear those **hypocritical** smiles no longer! I felt that I must scream or die!—and now—again!—hark! louder! louder! louder! *louder!*—

"**Villains**!" I shrieked, "**dissemble** no more! I admit the deed!—**tear up** the planks!—here, here!—it is the beating of his hideous heart"

---

pleasant ['pleznt] feundlich, nett **make a mockery of** ['mɒkərɪ] Spott treiben mit **agony** ['ægənɪ] (Höllen)Qual **derision** [dɪ'rɪʒn] Hohn, Spott **hypocritical** [hɪpəʊ'krɪtɪkəl] heuchlerisch, scheinheilig **villain** ['vɪlən] Schurke **dissemble** [dɪ'sembl] sich verstellen **tear up** [teə] herausreißen

The Cask of Amontillado

By *Edgar Allan Poe*

The thousand **injuries** of Fortunato I had **borne** as I best could, but when he **ventured** upon **insult**, I vowed **revenge**. You, who so well know the nature of my soul, will not suppose, however, that I **gave utterance** to a threat. *At length* I would be **avenged**; this was a point definitely **settled**—but the very definitiveness with which it was **resolved**, **precluded** the idea of risk. I must not only punish, but punish **with impunity**. A wrong is **unredressed** when **retribution** overtakes its **redresser**. It is equally unredressed when the avenger **fails to make** himself felt as to him who has done the wrong.

It must be understood that neither by word nor deed had I given Fortunato cause to doubt my good will. I continued as was my **wont**, to smile in his face, and he did not **perceive** that my smile *now* was at the thought of his **immolation**.

He had a weak point-this Fortunato—although in other **regards** he was a man to be respected and even feared. He **prided himself** on his **connoisseurship** in wine. Few Italians have the true **virtuoso spirit**. For the most part their en-

---

cask [kɑːsk] Fass **amontillado** [əmɒntɪ'lɑːdəʊ] Amontillado (heller, herber Sherry) **injury** ['ɪndʒərɪ] Kränkung **borne** [bɔːn] von **bear** [beə] ertragen, erdulden **venture** ['ventʃə] (es) wagen **insult** ['ɪnsʌlt] persönliche Beleidigung **revenge** [rɪ'vendʒ] Rache **gave utterance to** ['ʌtərəns] von **give utterance to** aussprechen, äußern **avenge** [ə'vendʒ] rächen **settled** ['setld] beschlossen **resolve** [rɪ'zɒlv] beschließen **preclude** [prɪ'kluːd] ausschließen **with impunity** [ɪm'pjuːnɪtɪ] (hier: selbst) ungestraft **unredressed** ['ʌnrɪ'drest] nicht vergolten, ungesühnt **retribution** [retrɪ'bjuːʃn] Vergeltung, Bestrafung **redresser** [rɪ'dresə] der das Unrecht Wiedergutmachende **fail to do s.th.** [feɪl] etwas nicht fertig bringen **wont** [wəʊnt] Gewohnheit, Art **perceive** [pə'siːv] (be)merken **immolation** [ɪməʊ'leɪʃn] Opferung **regard** [rɪ'gɑːd] Hinsicht **pride o.s. on s.th.** [praɪd] stolz sein auf etwas **connoisseurship** [kɒnə'sɜːʃɪp] Kennerschaft **virtuoso** [vɜːtjʊ'əʊzəʊ] Kunstliebhaber **spirit** ['spɪrɪt] Einstellung

thusiasm is **adapted** to **suit** the time and opportunity—to **practise imposture upon** the British and Austrian millionaires. In painting and **gemmary** Fortunato, like his countrymen, was a **quack**—but in the matter of old wines he was **sincere**. In this respect I did not differ from him **materially**: I was **skilful in** the Italian **vintages** myself, and bought largely whenever I could.

It was about **dusk**, one evening during the supreme madness of the carnival season, that I encountered my friend. He **accosted me** with excessive warmth, for he had been drinking much. The man wore **motley**. He had on a tight-fitting **parti-striped** dress, and his head was surmounted by the **conical** cap and bells. I was so pleased to see him, that I thought I should never **have done wringing** his hand.

I said to him: "My dear Fortunato, you are luckily met. How remarkably well you are looking today! But I have received a **pipe** of what **passes for** Amontillado, and I have my doubts."

"How?" said he. "Amontillado? A pipe? Impossible! And in the middle of the carnival!"

"I have my doubts," I replied; "and I was silly enough to pay the full Amontillado price without consulting you in the matter. You were not to be found, and I was **fearful of** losing a bargain."

---

be adapted [ə'dæptɪd] angewendet werden **suit** [sju:t] sich anpassen **practise imposture upon s.o.** ['præktɪs ɪm'pɒstʃə] j-n betrügen od. hereinlegen **gemmary** ['dʒemərɪ] (Gebiet der) Edelsteine **quack** [kwæk] prahlerischer Dilettant, Scharlatan **sincere** [sɪn'sɪə] aufrichtig, hier: ernst zu nehmen **materially** [mə'tɪərɪəlɪ] wesentlich **be skilful in** ['skɪlfʊl] sich verstehen auf **vintage** ['vɪntɪdʒ] guter Wein **dusk** [dʌsk] Abenddämmerung **accost s.o.** [ə'kɒst] j-n ansprechen od. begrüßen **motley** ['mɒtlɪ] Narrenkostüm **parti-striped** ['pɑ:tɪstraɪpt] bunt gestreift **conical** ['kɒnɪkəl] spitz **have done doing s.th.** mit etwas aufhören **wring s.o.'s hand** [rɪŋ] j-m die Hand drücken **pipe** [paɪp] großes Weinfass **pass for s.th.** [pɑ:s] angeblich etwas sein, etwas sein sollen **be fearful** ['fɪəfʊl] Angst haben, fürchten

"Amontillado!"
"I have my doubts."
"Amontillado!"
"And I must satisfy them."
"Amontillado!"
"As you are **engaged**, I am on my way to Luchesi. If anyone has a **critical turn**, it is he. He will tell me—"
"Luchesi cannot **tell** Amontillado **from** Sherry."
"And yet some fools will have it that his taste is a **match** for your own."
"Come, let us go."
"**Whither**?"
"To your **vaults**."
"My friend, no; I will not **impose upon your good nature**. I perceive you have an engagement. Luchesi—"
"I have no engagement; come."
"My friend, no. It is not the engagement, but the severe cold with which I perceive you are **afflicted**. The vaults are insufferably damp. They are **encrusted** with **nitre**."
"Let us go, nevertheless. The cold is merely nothing. Amontillado! You have been imposed upon. And as for Luchesi, he cannot distinguish Sherry from Amontillado."
Thus speaking, Fortunato **possessed himself of** my arm. Putting on a mask of black silk, and drawing a ***roquelaire***

---

be engaged [ɪn'geɪdʒd] etwas vorhaben, keine Zeit haben **have a critical turn** ['krɪtɪkəl tɜːn] hier: sich auskennen **tell s.th. from s.th.** etwas von etwas unterscheiden können **be a match for s.o.** [mætʃ] es mit j-m aufnehmen können **whither** ['wɪðə] wohin **vault** [vɔːlt] Weinkeller, Kellergewölbe **impose upon s.o.'s good nature** [ɪm'pəʊz, 'neɪtʃə] j-s Gutmütigkeit ausnützen **be afflicted with** [ə'flɪktɪd] leiden an **be encrusted** [ɪn'krʌstɪd] bedeckt sein **nitre** ['naɪtə] Salpeter **possess o.s. of s.th.** [pə'zes] hier: etwas ergreifen **roquelaire** [rɒkə'leə] franz. weiter Mantel

closely about my person, I **suffered** him to hurry me to my palazzo.

There were no **attendants** at home; they had **absconded** to **make merry** in honour of the time. I had told them that I should not return until the morning, and had given them explicit orders not to **stir** from the house. These orders were **sufficient**, I well knew, to **insure** their immediate disappearance, **one and all**, as soon as my back was turned.

I took from their **sconces** two **flambeaux**, and giving one to Fortunato, **bowed** him through several **suites of rooms** to the **archway** that led into the vaults. I passed down a long and **winding staircase**, requesting him to be cautious as he followed. We came at length to the foot of the descent, and stood together on the damp ground of the catacombs of the Montresors.

The **gait** of my friend was unsteady, and the bells upon his cap **jingled** as he **strode**.

"The pipe?" said he.

"It is further on," said I; "but observe the white **webwork** which gleams from these **cavern** walls."

He turned towards me, and looked into my eyes with two **filmy orbs** that **distilled** the **rheum** of **intoxication**.

"Nitre?" he asked, at length.

"Nitre!" I replied, "How long have you had that cough?"

---

suffer s.o. to do s.th. ['sʌfə] j-n etwas tun lassen **attendant** [ə'tendənt] Diener; Pl Dienerschaft **abscond** [əb'skɒnd] sich heimlich davonmachen **make merry** ['merɪ] lustig sein, sich amüsieren **stir** [stɜː] sich rühren **be sufficient** [sə'fɪʃnt] genügen **insure** [ɪn'ʃʊə] garantieren **one and all** ohne Ausnahme **sconce** [skɒns] Halter **flambeau** ['flæmbəʊ] Fackel **bow s.o. through s.th.** [baʊ] j-n unter Verbeugungen durch etwas geleiten **suite of rooms** [swiːt] Zimmerflucht **archway** ['ɑːtʃweɪ] Bogengang **winding staircase** ['waɪndɪŋ 'steəkeɪs] Wendeltreppe **gait** [geɪt] Gang **jingle** ['dʒɪŋgl] klingeln **strode** [strəʊd] von **stride** [straɪd] steif gehen, stelzen **webwork** ['webwɜːk] Flor, pelzartige Oberfläche **cavern** ['kævən] Höhle **filmy** ['fɪlmɪ] verschleiert, trübe **orb** [ɔːb] (poetisch:) Auge **distill** [dɪs'tɪl] herauströpfeln lassen **rheum** [ruːm] Tränen, Wasser **intoxication** [ɪntɒksɪ'keɪʃn] Trunkenheit

"Ugh! ugh! ugh!—ugh! ugh! ugh!—ugh! ugh! ugh!—ugh! ugh! ugh!—ugh! ugh! ugh!

My poor friend found it impossible to reply for many minutes.

"It is nothing," he said, at last.

"Come," I said, with decision, "we will go back; your health is **precious**. You are rich, respected, admired, beloved; you are happy, as once I was. You are a man to be missed. For me it is no matter. We will go back; you will be ill, and I cannot be responsible. Besides, there is Luchesi—"

"Enough," he said; "the cough is a mere nothing; it will not kill me. I shall not die of a cough."

"True—true," I replied; "and, indeed, I had no intention of **alarming** you unnecessarily—but you should use all **proper precautions**. A **draught** of this **Medoc** will **defend us from** the damps."

Here I knocked off the neck of a bottle which I drew from a long row of its **fellows** that lay upon the **mould**.

"Drink," I said, **presenting** him the wine.

He raised it to his lips with a **leer**. He paused and nodded to me familiarly, while his bells jingled.

"I drink," he said, "to **the buried** that **repose** around us."

"And I to your long life."

He again took my arm, and we proceeded.

---

precious ['preʃəs] kostbar **alarm** [ə'lɑːm] beunruhigen **proper** ['prɒpə] geeignet **precaution** [prɪ'kɔːʃn] Vorsichtsmaßnahme **draught** [drɑːft] Schluck **Medoc** ['medɒk] Medoc (französische Weinsorte) **defend s.o. from** [dɪ'fend] j-n schützen vor **fellows** Pl ['feləʊz] hier: gleichartige Flaschen, Flaschen derselben Sorte **mould** [məʊld] Sims **present s.o. s.th.** [prɪ'zent] j-m etwas reichen **leer** [lɪə] gieriger Blick **the buried** ['berɪd] die Begrabenen **repose** [rɪ'pəʊz] ruhen, begraben sein

"These vaults," he said, "are extensive."

"The Montresors," I replied, "were a great and numerous family."

"I forget your **arms**."

"A huge human foot **d'or**, in a **field azure**; the foot **crushes** a **serpent rampant** whose **fangs** are **imbedded in** the heel."

"And the motto?"

"***Nemo me impune lacessit***."

"Good!" he said.

The wine sparkled in his eyes and the bells jingled. My own **fancy** grew warm with the Medoc. We passed through walls of **piled** bones, with casks and **puncheons intermingling**, into the **inmost recesses** of the catacombs. I paused again, and this time I **made bold** to seize Fortunato by an arm above the elbow.

"The nitre," I said; "see, it increases. It hangs like moss upon the vaults. We are below the river's bed. The drops of **moisture trickle** among the bones. Come, we will go back **ere it** is too late. Your cough—"

"It is nothing," he said; "let us go on. But first, another draught of the Medoc."

I broke and reached him a **flagon** of De Grave. He emptied it **at a breath**. His eyes flashed with a **fierce** light. He laughed

---

arms Pl [ɑːmz] Wappen **d'or** [dɔː] (französisch:) golden **field** [fiːld] Feld, Grundfläche **azure** ['æʒə] azurblau **crush** [krʌʃ] zertreten **serpent** ['sɜːpənt] Schlange **rampant** ['ræmpənt] aufgerichtet **fang** [fæŋ] Giftzahn **be imbedded in** [ɪm'bedɪd] vergraben sein in **Nemo me impune lacessit!** lat. Niemand fordert mich ungestraft heraus! **fancy** ['fænsɪ] Phantasie **piled** [paɪld] aufgestapelt **puncheon** ['pʌntʃən] großes Weinfass **intermingling** [ɪntə(ː)'mɪŋlɪŋ] dazwischen verteilt **inmost** ['ɪnməʊst] tiefst, innerst **recess** [rɪ'ses] Winkel; Tiefe **make bold** [bəʊld] es wagen **moisture** ['mɔɪstʃə] Feuchtigkeit **trickle** ['trɪkl] sickern **ere** [eə] (poetisch:) ehe, bevor **flagon** ['flægən] bauchige Flasche **at a breath** [breθ] auf e-n Zug **fierce** [fɪəs] wild, leidenschaftlich

and threw the bottle **upward** with a gesticulation I did not understand.

I looked at him in surprise. He repeated the movement—a grotesque on.

"You do not comprehend?" he said.

"Not I," I replied.

"Then you are not of the brotherhood."

"How?"

"You are not the **masons**."

"Yes, yes," I said; "yes, yes."

"You? Impossible! A mason?"

"A mason," I replied.

"A sign," he said.

"It is this," I answered, **producing** a **trowel** from beneath the **folds** of my *roquelaire*.

"You **jest**," he exclaimed, **recoiling** a few **paces**."But let us proceed to the Amontillado."

"Be it so," I said, replacing the tool beneath the cloak, and again offering him my arm. He leaned upon it heavily. We continued our route in search of the Amontillado. We passed through a **range** of low **arches**, **descended**, passed on, and descending again, arrived at a deep **crypt**, in which the **foulness of the air** caused our flambeaux **rather** to glow than flame.

---

upward ['ʌpwəd] hoch **mason** ['meɪsn] Freimaurer; Maurer **produce** [prə'djuːs] hervorholen, herausziehen **trowel** ['traʊəl] Maurerkelle **fold** [fəʊld] Falte **jest** [dʒest] spotten **recoil** [rɪ'kɔɪl] zurückweichen **pace** [peɪs] Schritt **range** [reɪndʒ] Reihe **arch** [ɑːtʃ] (Gewölbe)Bogen **descend** [dɪ'send] hinuntergehen, tiefer steigen **crypt** [krɪpt] Gruft **foulness of the air** ['faʊlnɪs, eə] schlechte, sauerstoffarme Luft **rather** ['rɑːðə] eher

At the **most remote** end of the crypt there appeared another **less spacious**. Its walls had been **lined** with **human remains**, piled to the vault overhead, in the fashion of the great catacombs of Paris. Three sides of this interior crypt were still ornamented in this manner. From the fourth the bones had been thrown down, and lay **promiscuously** upon the earth, forming at one point a **mound** of some size. Within the wall thus **exposed** by the displacing of the bones, we perceived a **still interior** recess, in depth about four feet, in width three, in height six or seven. It seemed to have been constructed for no special **use within itself**, but formed **merely** the interval between two of the colossal **supports** of the roof of the catacombs, and was backed by one of their **circumscribing** walls of solid granite.

It was **in vain** that Fortunato, uplifting his **dull torch**, **endeavoured** to **pry into** the depth of the recess. Its **termination** the feeble light did not **enable** us to see.

"Proceed," I said; "herein is the Amontillado. As for Luchesi—"

"He is an **ignoramus**," interrupted my friend, as he stepped unsteadily forward, while I followed immediately at this heels. In an instant he had reached the extremity of the niche, and finding his progress **arrested** by the rock, stood stupidly **bewildered**. A moment more and I had **fettered**

---

most remote [rɪ'məʊt] entferntest, entlegenst, äußerst **less spacious** ['speɪʃəs] weniger groß, kleiner **line** [laɪn] einfassen **human remains** Pl [rɪ'meɪnz] menschliche Überreste **promiscuously** [prə'mɪskjʊəslɪ] kunterbunt durcheinander **mound** [maʊnd] Haufen, Berg **expose** [ɪks'pəʊz] freilegen **still interior** noch verborgener gelegen **use within itself** [juːs] Selbstzweck **merely** ['mɪəlɪ] nur, lediglich **support** [sə'pɔːt] Stützpfeiler **circumscribing** ['sɜːkəmskraɪbɪŋ] außen herumführend **in vain** [veɪn] vergeblich **dull** [dʌl] schwach, trübe **torch** [tɔːtʃ] Fackel **endeavour** [ɪn'devə] versuchen **pry into** [praɪ] zu erforschen suchen **termination** [tɜːmɪ'neɪʃn] (äußerstes) Ende **enable s.o.** [ɪ'neɪbl] es j-m möglich machen **ignoramus** [ɪgnə'reɪməs] Ignorant **arrest** [ə'rest] aufhalten **bewildered** [bɪ'wɪldəd] verwirrt **fetter** ['fetə] fesseln

him to the granite. In its surface were two iron **staples**, distant from each other about two feet, horizontally. From one of these **depended** a short chain, from the other a **padlock**. Throwing the **links** about his **waist**, it was but the work of a few seconds to secure it. He was too much **astounded** to resist. Withdrawing the key I stepped back from the recess.

"Pass your hand," I said, "over the wall; you **cannot help** feeling the nitre. Indeed it is *very* damp. Once more let me ***implore*** you to return. No? Then I must **positively** leave you. But I must first **render** you all the little **attentions** in my power."

"The Amontillado!" **ejaculated** my friend, not yet recovered from his astonishment.

"True," I replied; "the Amontillado."

As I said these words I **busied** myself among the pile of bones of which I have before spoken. Throwing them aside, I soon uncovered a **quantity** of **building stones** and **mortar**. With these materials and **with the aid** of my trowel, I began **vigorously** to **wall up** the entrance of the niche.

I had scarcely laid the first **tier** of the **masonry** when I discovered that the intoxication of Fortunato had **in a great measure worn off**. The earliest **indication** I had of this was a **low moaning** cry from the depth of the recess. It was *not* the cry of a drunken man. There was then a long and

---

staple ['steɪpl] Krampe **depend** [dɪ'pend] herabhängen **padlock** ['pædlɒk] Vorhängeschloss **links** Pl [lɪŋks] Fessel **waist** [weɪst] Taille **astounded** [əs'taʊndɪd] verblüfft **s.o. cannot help doing s.th.** j-d muss etwas tun **implore** [ɪm'plɔː] anflehen **positively** ['pɒzətɪvlɪ] wirklich **render s.o. attentions** ['rendə, ə'tenʃnz] j-m Aufmerksamkeiten erweisen **ejaculate** [ɪ'dʒækjʊleɪt] ausrufen **busy o.s.** ['bɪzɪ] sich zu schaffen machen **a quantity of** ['kwɒntɪtɪ] eine Anzahl von **building stone** ['bɪldɪŋ stəʊn] Mauerstein **mortar** ['mɔːtə] Mörtel **with the aid of** [eɪd] mit Hilfe **vigorous** ['vɪgərəs] tatkräftig **wall up** [wɔːl] zumauern **tier** [tɪə] Reihe, Schicht **masonry** ['meɪsnrɪ] Mauerwerk **in a great measure** ['meʒə] in großem Maße, beträchtlich **worn off** [wɔːn] von **wear off** [weə] nachlassen **indication** [ɪndɪ'keɪʃn] Anzeichen **low** [ləʊ] **schwach** **moaning** ['məʊnɪŋ] stöhnend

obstinate silence. I laid the second tier, and the third, and the fourth; and then I heard the furious vibrations of the chain. The noise lasted for several minutes, during which, that I might **hearken to** it with the more satisfaction, I **ceased** my labours and sat down upon the bones. When at last the **clanking subsided**, I resumed the trowel, and finished without interruption the fifth, the sixth, and the seventh tier. The wall was now nearly upon a level with my breast. I again paused, and holding the flambeaux over the mason-work, threw a few feeble **rays** upon the figure within.

A succession of loud and shrill screams, **bursting** suddenly from the throat of the chained form, seemed to thrust me violently back. For a brief moment I hesitated—I trembled. **Unsheathing** my **rapier**, I began to **grope** with it about the recess; but the thought of an instant **reassured** me. I placed my hand upon the solid **fabric** of the catacombs, and felt satisfied. I **reapproached** the wall. I replied to the **yells** of him who **clamoured**. I reechoed—I aided—I **surpassed** them in **volume** and in strength. I did this, and the clamourer grew still.

It was now midnight, and my task was **drawing to a close**. I had **completed** the eighth, the ninth, and the tenth tier. I had finished a portion of the last and the eleventh; there remained but a single stone to be **fitted** and **plastered in**. I

---

obstinate ['ɒbstɪnɪt] hartnäckig **hearken** ['hɑːkən] zuhören **cease** [siːz] aufhören mit **clanking** ['klæŋkɪŋ] Gerassel **subside** [səb'saɪd] sich legen **ray** [reɪ] Strahl **a succession of** [sək'seʃn] eine Reihe od. Folge von **burst from** [bɜːst] dringen aus **unsheathe** ['ʌn'ʃiːð] (aus der Scheide) ziehen **rapier** ['reɪpjə] Degen **grope** [grəʊp] herumtasten **reassure** [riːə'ʃʊə] beruhigen **fabric** ['fæbrɪk] Gefüge **reapproach** ['rɪə'prəʊtʃ] wieder gehen zu, sich wieder nähern **yell** [jel] (gellender) Schrei **clamour** ['klæmə] schreien **surpass** [sɜː'pɑːs] übertreffen **volume** ['vɒljʊm] Fülle **draw to a close** [drɔː, kləʊz] sich dem Ende nähern **complete** [kəm'pliːt] beenden **fit** [fɪt] einfügen **plaster in** ['plɑːstə] hier: einzementieren

struggled with its weight; I placed it partially in its **destined position**. But now there came from out the niche a low laugh that **erected the hairs upon my head**. It was **succeeded** by a sad voice, which I had difficulty in recognizing as that of the noble Fortunato. The voice said—

"Ha! ha! ha!—he! he!—a very good joke indeed—an excellent jest. We will have many a rich laugh about it at the palazzo—he! he! he!—over our wine—he! he! he!"

"The Amontillado!" I said.

"He" he! he!—he! he! he!—yes, the Amontillado. But is it not getting late? Will not they be awaiting us at the palazzo, the Lady Fortunato and the rest? Let us be gone."

"Yes," I said, "**let us be gone**."

"For the love of God, Montresor!"

"Yes," I said, "for the love of God!"

But to these words I hearkened in vain for a reply. I grew impatient. I called aloud.

"Fortunato!"

No answer. I called again:

"Fortunato!"

No answer still. I **thrust** a torch through the remaining **aperture** and let it fall within. There came forth in return only a jingling of the bells. My heart grew sick—**on account of** the dampness of the catacombs. I **hastened** to make an

---

struggle with ['strʌgl] sich abmühen mit, Mühe haben mit **destined position** ['destɪnd pə'zɪʃn] vorgesehene Lage **erect the hairs upon s.o.'s head** [ɪ'rekt] j-m die Haare zu Berge stehen lassen **be succeeded by** [sək'siːdɪd] abgelöst werden von **let us be gone** lass uns gehen **thrust** [θrʌst] werfen **aperture** ['æpətjʊə] Öffnung **on account of** [ə'kaʊnt] wegen **hasten** ['heɪsn] sich beeilen

end of my labour. I **forced** the last stone **into its position**; I plastered it up. Against the new masonry I re-erected the old **rampart** of bones. For the half of a century no mortal has disturbed them. ***In pace requiescat!***

---

force s.th. into its position [fɔːs] etwas mit aller Kraft in die richtige Lage bringen **rampart** ['ræmpɑːt] Wall **In pace requiescat!** lat. Er ruhe in Frieden!

Edgar Allan Poe

Edgar Allan Poe, American poet, short-story writer and critic, was born in 1809 in Boston. His parents were itinerant actors. Orphaned at the age of three Poe was taken into the home of John Allan who educated him in schools in England and Richmond, Virginia. Withdrawn from the University of Virginia because of his gambling debts Poe went to Boston, where his first volume of poetry was published anonymously in 1827. He enlisted in the army and later went to West Point Military Academy. But after less than a year he was dismissed for neglect of duty. In the meantime his second volume of poems appeared in 1829.

After years spent in Baltimore and Richmond, where he began to publish stories in magazines, Poe married his fourteen-year-old cousin in 1836 and in 1837 he went to New York. From 1838 to 1844 he lived in Philadelphia where he collected his "Tales of the Grotesque and Arabesque" (published in 1840), and where he edited two magazines. His criticism in these and other journals made him respected and feared. In 1844 Poe moved again to New York. "The Raven and Other Poems" published in 1845 brought him some fame. The appearance of a new collection of short stories in 1846 added even more to this fame. Nevertheless, until his death, Poe struggled against poverty, doing literary hack work and habitually taking to alcohol. In 1849 he was found in the streets of Baltimore, dying in a drunken stupor.

During his lifetime Poe was misunderstood as a man and writer. Literary critics regarded his work as that of a madman. But today, Poe is the most widely read of all American authors of the nineteenth century. Poe is read because he possessed one of the most original imaginations. Never before and rarely since has an author so wholly and impressively captured the special atmosphere which was such a masterful creation of Poe's. His ingenuity and analytic ability was extraordinary. Poe's roots lay in the romantic tale of horror combined with analysis. His stories may be said to fall into two categories: those of horror in which he explored the supernatural and abnormal with gripping suspense; and those of ratiocination which set the standard for the modern detective stories. In these stories each word is in place. The structure of every sentence contributes sharply to the ultimate effect. The climax of horror is reached in a state of genuine excitement.

Poe is the father of the detective story and his influence on the literature of many countries has been enormous. George Bernard Shaw called him "this finest of finest of artists". Sir Arthur Conan Doyle said, "... For those tales have been so pregnant with suggestion, so stimulating to the mind of others, that it may be said of many of them that each is a root from which a whole literature has developed." And Dorothy L. Sayers wrote about him, "... he gave us the working model of the Holmes-Watson combination and of that opposition between the conventional policeman and the unconventional amateur which was later to become a commonplace of detective fiction. He also established the two great formulae for the 'surprise' solution, by way of the unexpected means ('Murders in the Rue Morgue') and the most unlikely person ('Thou Art the Man'), and, in 'The Purloined Letter', pointed the way to the solution achieved by psychological, rather than material, clues." The latter story shows Poe's fine balance of the "intellectual" and the "sensational". "The Mystery of Marie Rogêt" is often thought not only Poe's outstanding achievement in the genre but also one of the best detective stories ever written. But "The Murders in the Rue Morgue" is historically the most important story, since it was the world's first detective story in a modern sense.

It should be recognized, however, that Poe did not think of himself as writing detective stories, the word detective was unknown at the time the first of these stories, "The Murders in the Rue Morgue", appeared. He did not regard these particular stories as of much importance.

In a letter to a friend Poe himself wrote about his stories, "... These tales of ratiocination ... owe most of their popularity to being something in a new key. I do not mean to say that they are not ingenious - but people think them more ingenious than they are - on account of their method and *air* of method ..."

Dorothy L. Sayers

Dorothy L. Sayers was born in 1893 at Oxford. She was educated at Salisbury and at Somerville College, Oxford, where she graduated in medieval literature in 1915. She took up writing as a career and her first novel appeared in 1923. She was probably best known for her Lord Peter Wimsey stories, but her religious plays, in particular "The Man Born to Be King", reached a wide public. She has made a verse translation of Dante's "Divine Comedy". Dorothy Sayers died in 1957.

For her admirers Dorothy Sayers is the finest detective story writer of the twentieth century. In reading her novels one must admire the careful craftsmanship with which they have been made. Her plots are organized with care, the details are often original and carefully researched. She was of the opinion that the stories must possess an "Aristotelian perfection of beginning, middle and end". They must be fair, accurate, interesting and well written, laying all the clues before the reader, and with an unexpected twist towards the end. Of great importance are the logical elements in the unravelling of the mystery.

Dorothy Sayers, tired of reiterated blunt instruments, devoted considerable ingenuity to devising new methods. As early as 1930 one A. Berkeley said, "I am personally convinced that ... the detective story is in the process of developing the novel with a detective or crime interest, holding its readers less by mathematical than by psychological ties. The puzzle element will no doubt remain, but it will become a puzzle of character rather than a puzzle of time, place, motive, and opportunity." Dorothy Sayers wrote in an essay on one of her books, "Gaudy Night", in 1937, "We also took occasion to preach at every opportunity that if the detective story was to live and develop it get back to where it began in the hands of Collins and Le Fanu, and become once more a novel of manners instead of a pure crossword puzzle."

In most of her novels and short stories the actual manner of the murder is not a major feature. Her books are, through clever characterization and description, at the same time novels and stories of character and manners, so that one critic could write about her, "The Wimsey books are for the most part better as novels than as detective novels; they have wit, humour, good charcter-drawing, and a quality of high seriousness imparted to them by the author's religious sense."

Lord Peter Wimsey, Dorothy Sayers' amateur detective, is a caricature of an English aristocrat, conceived with an immensely snobbish loving seriousness, "yet unique in character and methods". Phrases like the following, where Lord Peter talks to his dentist, are typical examples of his mannerism in speaking: "Oh, some of your whizz-bang business, I suppose ... Jolly old left-hand upper grinder come to bits on me ... Don't be silly, old horse ..." Or he says things like "I'll drop in on you later and we'll have a jolly old pow-wow, what?"

Over the years Wimsey remains essentially unchanged. But after "Busman's Honeymoon", published in 1937, and sub-titled. "A love story with detective interruptions", Dorothy Sayers turned away from the hero of whom she had said, "I can see no end to Peter this side of the grave".